NEW ERA
BUSINESS ENGLISH

新时代
商务英语综合教程

教师用书 3

总主编 王立非
主 编 周 平
副主编 方秀才 常 锟
原著作者 【英】Anne Williams
         【英】Louise Pile
         【英】Catrin Lloyd-Jones

清华大学出版社
北京

Copyright © 2013 Cengage Learning, Inc.

Original edition published by Cengage Learning, Inc. All Rights reserved.
本书原版由圣智学习出版公司出版。版权所有，盗印必究。

Tsinghua University Press is authorized by Cengage Learning to publish, distribute and sell exclusively this edition. This edition is authorized for sale in the People's Republic of China only (excluding Hong Kong SAR, Macao SAR and Taiwan). No part of this publication may be reproduced or distributed by any means, or stored in a database or retrieval system, without the prior written permission of Cengage Learning.
本改编版由圣智学习出版公司授权清华大学出版社独家出版发行。此版本仅限在中华人民共和国境内销售，不包括中国香港、澳门特别行政区及中国台湾省。未经授权的本书出口将被视为违反版权法的行为。未经出版者预先书面许可，不得以任何方式复制或发行本书的任何部分。

"National Geographic", "National Geographic Society" and the Yellow Border Design are registered trademarks of the National Geographic Society ® Marcas Registradas.

Cengage Learning Asia Pte. Ltd.
151 Lorong Chuan, #02-08 New Tech Park, Singapore 556741
本书封面贴有 Cengage Learning 防伪标签，无标签者不得销售。

北京市版权局著作权合同登记号　图字：01-2018-0757

版权所有，侵权必究。举报：010-62782989，beiqinquan@tup.tsinghua.edu.cn。

图书在版编目（CIP）数据

新时代商务英语综合教程. 教师用书. 3 / 王立非总主编；周平主编. —北京：清华大学出版社，2020.12
ISBN 978-7-302-53708-3

Ⅰ. ①新… Ⅱ. ①王… ②周… Ⅲ. ①商务—英语—高等学校—教学参考资料　Ⅳ. ①F7

中国版本图书馆 CIP 数据核字（2019）第 185502 号

责任编辑：徐　静
封面设计：子　一
责任校对：王凤芝
责任印制：丛怀宇

出版发行：清华大学出版社
　　网　　址：http://www.tup.com.cn，http://www.wqbook.com
　　地　　址：北京清华大学学研大厦A座　　邮　编：100084
　　社 总 机：010-62770175　　　　　　　　邮　购：010-62786544
　　投稿与读者服务：010-62776969，c-service@tup.tsinghua.edu.cn
　　质量反馈：010-62772015，zhiliang@tup.tsinghua.edu.cn
印 装 者：三河市龙大印装有限公司
经　　销：全国新华书店
开　　本：210mm×285mm　　　印　张：6.5　　　字　数：176千字
版　　次：2020年12月第1版　　　　　　　　　　印　次：2020年12月第1次印刷
定　　价：49.00元

产品编号：078734-01

Preface

改革开放 40 年，商务英语专业创办 10 年来，全国已有 393 所高校开设了商务英语本科专业，商务英语人才培养在我国已初具规模，商务英语人才培养体系不断完善，一个突出的标志就是核心课程和核心教材建设。近年来，商务英语专业教材建设的特点是：引进和原创相结合，引进了一批国际知名的经典商务英语教材，如 *Market Leader*、*Intelligent Business*、*Cambridge Business English Certificate* 等，而且，还自主开发了一批商务英语教材；其次是继承和创新相结合，在继承外语技能教学优良传统的同时，将语言、文化、商务相结合，解决了打牢英语基本功、学习文化、培养商务意识和商务素养兼顾的难题；此外，教材和课程建设同步，通过编写教材，创建了"综合商务英语"等一批新课，打造出"金课"，有力地推动了商务英语专业核心课程和教材建设。

根据 2018 年教育部颁布的《普通高等学校外国语言文学类本科专业教学质量国家标准》的要求，商务英语专业必须开设 17 门核心课程，其中最重要的一门课程就是"综合商务英语"。该课程是商务英语专业基础阶段的英语技能主干课程，对打牢学生的商务英语基本功、拓展商务文化、培养商务意识和商务素养极为重要。

针对"综合商务英语"主干核心课程，清华大学出版社引进了著名的剑桥商务英语经典教材，并按国家标准的要求，组织强大的商务英语教材编写团队，经过精心改编，推出了"新时代商务英语综合教程"。这套教材具有以下六个特点：

第一，原版引进著名的剑桥商务英语教材，该教材编写和出版质量高，在国外面世后多次再版，多年畅销，经久不衰，堪称经典。

第二，改编后的教材共分为 4 册，适合 1~2 年级"综合商务英语"课程 4 个学期使用，每学期使用 1 册。每册 8 个单元，4 册共 32 个单元，每个单元包含 2 篇课文，适合每周 4

个学时的课堂教学使用。

  第三，所有单元的主题都与真实职场和商务活动密切相关，并经过精心编排，教材主题由浅入深，既相互联系，又相对独立。课文选材短小精悍，图文并茂，语篇鲜活，可读性极强，并配有充足的练习题，练习任务设计丰富而实用，兼顾词汇、语法、听说、写作、翻译、商务知识、商务文化、商务沟通等各方面。

  第四，对引进教材做适当改编，以符合中国英语教学的特点和需求。此外，还增加了全英文的商务知识点和商务翻译，前者扩展学生的商务知识，后者训练学生英汉互译的能力，弥补了教材背景知识不足、没有翻译练习的缺陷。

  第五，为第 3 册和第 4 册教材精心编配了商务案例分析单元，训练学生以问题为导向，以案例为对象，提高商务环境下分析问题和解决问题的能力。

  第六，针对全国商务英语专业四级考试的题型和要求，教材练习部分增加了与四级考试相关的题型，帮助学生熟悉和了解四级考试的形式和难度。

  本套教材适合全国商务英语专业应用型本科院校作为"综合商务英语"课程教材使用，也适合高职高专商务英语专业选用，同时也可作为经管类专业学生的专业英语教材，以及商务英语爱好者和企业员工英语培训使用。本套教材的改编得到了对外经济贸易大学、西南财经大学、华中农业大学、山东财经大学、安徽财经大学等高校的专家和清华大学出版社的领导和编辑的大力支持，在此表示衷心感谢。

  谨以此纪念改革开放 40 年商务英语的发展，是为序。

北京语言大学教授、博士生导师

王立非

2019年1月于北京

Contents

Unit 1 Teamwork 1
Unit 2 Corporate hospitality 11
Unit 3 Public relations 21
Unit 4 Ordering goods 31
Review Test 1 39
Unit 5 Relocation 45
Unit 6 Work safety and rights 53
Unit 7 Business expenses 63
Unit 8 Staff appraisal 73
Case study Cash flow 83
Review Test 2 91

Unit 1 Teamwork

> **Objectives**
>
> To enable Ss to talk about teams and teamwork
> To learn about working on managerial skills

Essential vocabulary

Teamwork	Training	General
accountable	to agree on (objectives)	advertisement
to allocate (roles)	approach	attitude
to assign (tasks)	benefit	convenient
to contribute / make a contribution	to bring in (a consultant)	effective
to co-operate	to come up with (ideas)	expatriate
to take on (responsibility)	to measure (progress)	honest
to trust	to set (targets)	to make (arrangements)
	survival course	schedule
	to work on (managerial skills)	subsidiary
	to work towards (objectives)	under pressure

Warming up

Task 1 Ss work in pairs and rank the characteristics of a good team.

Task 2 Ss focus on the aspects they have personally experienced and whether these have led to the success of the team.

> **Alternative activity**
> Alternatively, if such an activity is not too sensitive, T asks Ss to use the list of characteristics as a questionnaire and to ask each other questions in pairs about a specific team (e.g. *Do you all work towards a common objective?*). T asks Ss to score their partner's answer as follows:
> 3 = always   2 = sometimes   1 = rarely   0 = never
> T then elicits the scores and reads out feedback from the following:
> **Team assessment results**
> **0–14:** Are you sure you work in a team or just in a room with a group of other people? It sounds as if communication isn't a problem in your team; it just doesn't exist.
> **15–25:** Your team probably works quite happily together and could even be fairly productive. But have you ever stopped to ask yourselves what your values and objectives are? With a little more thought, your team could become a truly high-performance unit.

26–36: Congratulations! Your team is an effective, high-performance unit that should produce great results.

T and Ss then discuss how effective this assessment is and whether it corresponds with Ss' perceptions of their teams.

Text A

Comprehension tasks

Task 1

Suggested answers
1. d   2. a   3. c

Task 2

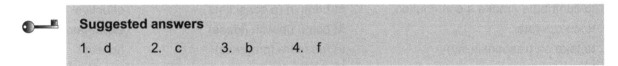

Suggested answers
1. d   2. c   3. b   4. f

Vocabulary

Task 3 Ss match verbs, prepositions and nouns from the text. Obviously, Ss should use each preposition more than once. T asks Ss to check their answers by referring back to the article. T ensures that Ss realise that these verbs can be used more broadly by eliciting other nouns, e.g. take on responsibility / a new job / additional duties, bring in a consultant / an expert, put on discos / events/plays.

Suggested answers
2. take on responsibility
3. bring in a consultant
4. work on managerial skills
5. come up with ideas
6. sell at a profit
7. look for people

Task 4

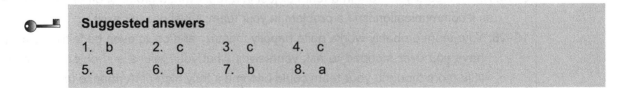

Suggested answers
1. b   2. c   3. c   4. c
5. a   6. b   7. b   8. a

Task 5

Suggested answers

2. chief executive (CEO)
3. brainstorming
4. counter-productive
5. decision-making
6. points of view
7. unanimous
8. casting vote
9. summary
10. minutes

Listening

Task 6

Suggested answers

1. b   2. g   3. c   4. h   5. e

Audioscripts

Call 1

Hello Frida. This is Margaret Brock here. It's 9:30 on Wednesday morning. I'm ringing about the half-year sales report. Could you send me a copy of your department's figures, please? I'm in Helsinki until Friday. Thanks very much. Bye.

Call 2

This is Frank Larsen from Scandinavian Conferences in Copenhagen. I'm ringing to tell you that this year's Danish Telecommunications Trade Fair's taking place in the week of November 22. If you'd like some complimentary tickets, please let me know how many you'll need. Please call me on 0045 33 346 766. Thank you. Bye.

Call 3

Hi Frida. It's Sue Mellor. How are you? I hope you're not too busy at the moment. I want to talk to you about my visit next month. You know we'd talked about the 13th? Well, I'm afraid it's not going to work out because of deadlines here. I don't suppose we could put it back a week or so, could we? Give me a ring and let me know. Thanks.

Call 4

Hi Frida. It's Colin. I'm on my mobile because I'm travelling to a meeting with a client but I need to talk to you urgently so could you call me on 0486 772 444? It's my mobile number. I need to talk to you about that contract we're trying to get in Helsinki because the customer accepted our proposal and I need to know whether it's all right if I just go ahead and sign the contracts or whether you want to get involved, as well. Could you get back to me ASAP? Thanks.

Call 5

Hello Frida. It's Steve Montgomery here. I got your proposal for the product launch and I've finally managed to get a look at it. It looks OK, but I think there could still be one or two minor problems with it. I think the time schedule looks a bit on the optimistic side, as well. I've got a couple of suggestions, which I'll get off to you today. Let me know what you think, OK? Bye.

Task 7 T asks Ss to read through the forms to check what type of information they are looking for. Ss listen and write in the missing information. In the first form T should alert Ss to the fact that in gap (4) they should not write more than two words or numbers. Therefore, only the following are acceptable: Tuesday 23 or 23 November.

> **Suggested answers**
> (1) Trade Fair   (2) S-126 25
> (3) 3   (4) Tuesday 23 / 23 November
> (5) (Kati) Gersel   (6) the/your message
> (7) cancelled   (8) not available
> (9) 27 November   (10) confirm

Audioscripts

Conversation 1

Tom   Good afternoon. Scandinavian Conferences.
Frida Good afternoon. Could I speak to Frank Larsen, please?
Tom   I'm afraid he's not here today. Can I help you?
Frida I'm ringing about the Danish Telecommunications Trade Fair. Mr. Larsen phoned to offer me some tickets and he asked me to let him know how many I'd need.
Tom   Well, I can send you the tickets. That's no problem. I'll just need your name and address.
Frida Right. It's Frida Andersson from Sanderlin. The address is Torshamnsgatan, S-126 25 Stockholm.
Tom   So, that's Frida Andersson at Torhamnsgatan, S-126 25. OK. How many tickets do you need?
Frida Three, please.
Tom   And which days would you like them for?
Frida Just for Tuesday 23 November, please.
Tom   And could I have the other names for the tickets?
Frida I'm afraid I can only confirm two names at the moment. Kati Gersel and myself.
Tom   Could you spell Gersel, please?
Frida Yes, that's G-E-R-S-E-L.
Tom   Right. I'll put the tickets in the post today.
Frida Thanks very much. Bye.
Tom   Thank you for calling. Goodbye.

Conversation 2

Receptionist	Good afternoon. Can I help you?
Frida	Good afternoon. Could I speak to Sue Mellor, please?
Receptionist	May I ask who's calling?
Frida	It's Frida Andersson from Head Office.
Receptionist	One moment, please. I'll put you through.
Receptionist	Hello?
Frida	Hello?
Receptionist	I'm afraid she's not in her office at the moment. Can I take a message?
Frida	Yes. Could you tell her that I got her message and I've cancelled our meeting on the 13th? But I'm not available the following week, so I suggest meeting on 27 November.
Receptionist	OK. So, that's Frida Andersson from Head Office. The meeting on the 13th is cancelled and you suggest meeting on 27 November instead.
Frida	That's right. And could she call me to confirm the date?
Receptionist	OK. I'll give her the message and she'll get back to you as soon as possible.
Frida	Thank you.
Receptionist	Oh, does she have your number?
Frida	Yes, she does.
Receptionist	OK. Thanks for calling.
Frida	Thanks. Bye.

Business communication

Task 8

Suggested answers

A team leader or team lead is someone (or in certain cases there may be multiple team leaders) who provides guidance, instruction, direction and leadership to a group of other individuals (the team) for the purpose of achieving a key result or group of aligned results. The team leader reports to a project manager who oversees several teams.

Qualities a team leader should possess include:
- Ability to get on well with colleagues;
- A good personal image;
- Technical knowledge;
- Experience of management;
- Ability to make people laugh;
- Willingness to work up to 60 hours a week;
- Ability to make difficult decisions under pressure;
- Concerning for the well-being of every employee;

- Ability to understand the details of company activities;
- Adaptability, such as coping with change; adjusting to new assignments; switching strategies rapidly; revising plans;
- Knowledge of the world;
- Highly educated and cultured individual with wide range of personal interest;
- Commitment to making money;
- Stable health and psychological make-up;
- Ability to motivate;
- Ability to delegate.

Translation

Task 9

Suggested answers

1. 当皮特·韦尔奇来到库松公司在波兰新收购的工厂并接任其首席执行官时，他发现那里的员工团队意识淡薄。
2. 在过去，所有事情，无论是要休假一天还是重大投资决定，都得请示负责人，所以在他办公室门外排队的人接连不断。
3. 这些举措也形成了每周例行检查的基础，通过检查来确保工作进展与项目所设定的目标一致。
4. 合作伙伴关系不仅能够增加获得人才的渠道、提升技术等级、分担投资，而且能让零售商以其个人无法实现的步伐向前发展。
5. 因为美国试图阻挠中国获得关键技术，中国正在资助旨在建立自己的垂直供应链的相关举措。

Task 10

Suggested answers

1. Due to the huge cultural differences and a lack of adequate communication between the two countries, negotiations have been difficult, which makes it difficult for China to acquire the Brazilian iron ore company.
2. All countries made a consensus that both developed and developing countries should be held accountable for global warming, and strive to reach their own targets of emission reduction through extensive dialogue and collaboration.
3. This giant state-owned enterprise, with 6,500 employees, has initiated a new recruitment programme in the hope that it will recruit as many as about 200 qualified engineers and maintenance staff.
4. It is estimated that the company will have a turnover of 4 trillion yuan this year, and that number will continue to rise in the future.
5. Reading CVs carefully will throw some light on the basic information of job applicants, thus helping interviewers better assess them, and ultimately select the best.

Task 11

> **Suggested answer**
>
> Dear Mr. Richardson,
>
> I am afraid you might have also noticed that there is a lack of co-operation in certain teams in our company and it has caused some problems such as work grievance and in-fighting, which has affected our work recently. Hereby, I am writing to make some humble suggestions on improving the concept of teamwork in our staff.
>
> First, in light of the current situation, team leaders and managers should be encouraged to communicate more with their team members. Weekly team meetings should be done routinely so that the staff have a chance to speak.
>
> Secondly, working on managerial skills should be stressed. Regular training sessions should be in place to improve the team work awareness and skills of managers from different levels.
>
> Last, appropriate policies should be taken to reward team-work actions.
>
> We do hope that those above can be taken into serious consideration and the situation will be better.
>
> Best regards,
> David Alan

Text B

Comprehension tasks

Task 1

> **Suggested answers**
> 1. Five.
> 2. London in the week of 9 February.
> 3. To build the team and agree on objectives, roles and schedules for the launch. They also need to discuss communication.
> 4. ASAP (as soon as possible).
> 5. The type of training to choose.

Task 2

> **Suggested answers**
> 1. False   The company must be headquartered in U.S.
> 2. True
> 3. False   They haven't been rejected.
> 4. False   It doesn't sell package holidays, but provides management training programmes.

5. False — This statement is not mentioned in the text.
6. True

Vocabulary

Task 3

Suggested answers
2. negotiate a deal
3. authorise a payment
4. submit a report
5. control costs
6. cast a vote
7. reorganise the company structure
8. delegate a task

Task 4

Suggested answers
2. e　3. a　4. g　5. h　6. f　7. d　8. c

Task 5

Suggested answers

verb	noun	person	adjective
manager	management	manager	managerial
administer	administration	administrator	administrative
assist	assistance	assistant	assistant
organise	organisation	organiser	organisational
partner	partnership	partner	partner
represent	representation	representative	representative
analyse	analysis	analyst	analytical
supervise	supervision	supervisor	supervisory

2. representative
3. supervisory
4. analytical
5. administration
6. partnership
7. assist
8. organisational

Speaking

Task 6 Ss discuss other companies they know of where teamwork has been successful. This task can be easier if T allows Ss to discuss people they know of doing good teamwork, such as their class monitor or tutor. This can be expanded to methods of working in class as a team and coming up with ideas to help each other.

Task 7 To lead into Task 7, T briefly asks Ss if they have taken part in any team-building courses and, if so, in what ways they and their team benefited from the course. Then, Ss discuss critical issues and set the priorities, if possible. Ss need to elaborate on their reasons.

Business communication

Task 8 Ss read the advertisements for the team-building courses. In pairs Ss discuss which course would suit the Carmichael team (mentioned in Text B) best and why. T asks Ss which course they chose and how it would benefit the five team members and the project. Ss then discuss which programme they would prefer, and why.

Translation

Task 9

Suggested answers

1. 两位推荐人选看起来都非常出色,并且我相信他们将会很好地与三位当地员工携手合作。
2. 这个团队将首先花几天时间参加团队建设活动,接下来讨论发布会相关问题。
3. 或者,如果你认为这样做更好的话,我们会邀请一位顾问来给我们开一个更传统的研讨会。
4. 特朗普总统不顾业界的反对和国会对白宫这项提案的不满,依然坚持威胁将全面加征对进口汽车的关税,希望以此方式让贸易伙伴国作出让步。
5. 到 2015 年为止,中国出口商品占全世界出口商品的比重为 13.76%,这个数字远远超过排名第二的美国,其占全球出口商品的比重为 9.1%。

Task 10

Suggested answers

1. A mini profile should be concise and focused to be appealing, and, attached with a link to one's personal website, if there is one.
2. Any summary or excerpt of this report does not represent the official viewpoints, which should be based on a complete version. If necessary, the client can contact the company's investment consultant for further advice.
3. The three-day seminar for domestic scholars focused on how to improve the service efficiency of cross-border e-commerce in China.
4. Once the user forgets the login password, he can retrieve it with the help of his registered mailbox, or alternatively, by answering preset security questions.

5. Building the Silk Road Economic Belt and the 21st-Century Maritime Silk Road (the Belt and Road) must be based on the reality of the region. The policymakers should seriously give some thought to the local economic, social, ethnic and religious characteristics and natural conditions.

Writing

Task 11

Suggested answer

Jim,

Could you please contact Team-Plus to organise a team-building event for sales staff? There would be eight participants and the course should last for two days. I suggest the weekend of 24/25 November or, if that is not possible, the following weekend.

Please send me your reply as soon as possible.

Thanks,
Alan

Unit 2 Corporate hospitality

Objectives

To enable Ss to talk about corporate hospitality
To practise reading for gist and specific information
To review language for dealing with invitations
To practise writing a letter of acceptance

Essential vocabulary

Entertaining	General
accommodation	to bring up (a subject)
to chat	contract
to establish/build (a relationship)	convenient
fact-finding mission	corporate event
to get down (to business)	delighted
to meet (expenses) to	to finalise (details)
round (of golf)	grateful
shopping trip	I look forward to…
sightseeing tour	to miss (an opportunity)
sociable	personal assistant (PA)
social setting	to place (an order)
sports event	purpose(ful)
(poor) timing	to set (objectives)
valued customer	substantial
	suitable

Warming up

Task 1   Ss read the profiles of the business people and match each profile with a way of entertaining them from the list. T elicits suggestions and reasons for Ss' choices.

Task 2   Ss first read through the entertaining activities and then form small groups to decide about the most popular one(s) to entertain clients in China. As Ss work, T should not guide Ss' choices but help them discuss the advantages or disadvantages of each activity. If possible, Ss discuss the cultural character in typical Chinese ways of entertaining guests.

Text A

Comprehension tasks

Task 1

Suggested answers

1. False — "Effective Social Influencing" is a training programme by Huthwaite.
2. False — Not always good, and timing is important.
3. True
4. True
5. False — Corporate events are not only for connecting people but also for discussing business.
6. False — It is a success when the goal of event is attained.

Task 2

Suggested answers

1. c   2. g   3. f   4. d

Vocabulary

Task 3

Suggested answers

2. a fact-finding mission
3. a trade fair
4. a sightseeing tour
5. a shopping trip
6. a sports event

Task 4

Suggested answers

verb	noun	person
partner	partnership	partner
claim	claim	claimant
negotiate	negotiation	negotiator
consume	consumption	consumer
distribute	distribution	distributor
host	host	host

2. negotiate
3. host
4. distribution
5. claimants
6. consumption

Task 5

Suggested answers

meet: customers, objectives
win: customers, orders, contracts
establish: relationships, objectives
cancel: orders, contracts
manage: customers, relationships

Listening

Task 6

Suggested answers
1. d   2. b   3. h   4. f   5. a

Audioscripts

1. Fine, thanks. I'm glad you managed to find me somewhere so near the office. That makes things so much easier in the morning. But I have to say, the bed was so hard I didn't get to sleep till two this morning.
2. Pretty awful, actually. There was one delay after another and then I got stopped at Customs. And apparently, my luggage is somewhere between here and Cape Town.
3. Wonderful. I'm really enjoying it here and the people are so friendly. I'll definitely come back for a holiday. But I'll need a week at least next time. Actually, I wouldn't mind living here for a while.
4. Well, I thought it was pretty good from our point of view, but I can see that some people might not be so happy. Still, we got through quite a lot and made some progress. But I still think we're a long way from a decision.
5. OK, but it was a bit too heavy for me. Actually, given a choice, I'd have preferred a salad.

Task 7 Ss first go through those techniques of encouraging conversation and then listen and fill in the blanks.

Audioscripts

Speaker 1	So, what did you think of the food?
Speaker 2	OK, but it was a bit too heavy for me. Actually, given a choice, I'd have preferred a salad.
Speaker 1	Salad?
Speaker 2	Oh, yes. I don't really eat meat.
Speaker 1	What do you have at home? You're not a vegetarian, are you?
Speaker 2	Well, I'm not. But my wife is.
Speaker 1	Oh, really?
Speaker 2	Oh, yes. I haven't had meat at home for years.
Speaker 1	Don't you miss it?
Speaker 2	Sometimes. But then I go and have a secret steak.

Business communication

Task 8 Warmer (books closed): T asks Ss what they think would be necessary in a good business hotel. When Ss have brainstormed a few ideas, T tells them to open their books and look at the criteria listed on the customer satisfaction form. Ss read the customer satisfaction form and decide on the three most important criteria for them. Ss give reasons for their choice.

Translation

Task 9

Suggested answers

1. 荷士卫是一家来自英国的培训顾问公司，这家公司量身定做的培训项目名为"有效的社会影响"，能够为您提供在社会环境下进行商务策划和经营所需要的知识和技巧，同时还能让你的顾客和潜在顾客都感到满意。
2. 这个课程所强调的第一件事就是，你所喜欢的活动并非能帮你达成目标的理想活动。
3. 根据荷士卫的观点，成功的秘诀和建立良好的商务关系的关键在于把你花在社交活动上的时间看作是去"影响"他人，而不是去做推销。
4. 与此同时，酒店业的繁荣使得这个行业不得不努力去吸引更多的员工，而行业里的高管们则抱怨许多酒店管理专业的毕业生流失到了其他行业。
5. 有了更加灵活的劳动力模型来帮助我们在任何时间、任何地点获取所需人才，我们现在能更好地应付不断变化的客户要求和需求。

Task 10

Suggested answers

1. This beer producer provides products for many restaurants with images of their own country's players and elements of the World Cup, making available a festive atmosphere of watching the games for fans and elevating beer brand's favourability at the same time.
2. China Construction Bank will continue to practise its mission and duties as the promoter of RMB internationalisation and the market leader, adhere to serving the entity economy, and provide tailor-made financial services for middle and small-sized enterprises.
3. Apart from exhibiting good sales prospects to the partners, outstanding suppliers should also seek to establish strategic partnership with them to discuss and solve business difficulties, and to provide the necessary financial and logistic support.
4. Hainan Province, which possesses an extraordinary geographic position and rich natural resources, is an important strategic supporting point for building the 21st-Century Maritime Silk Road, and the issue of the series of policies brings up a good timing for its development.
5. The Shanghai Municipal People's Government has sent a delegation to Guangzhou to specially arrange for the summit forum of medical cooperation which is to be held recently.

Writing

Task 11

Suggested answer

Re: Order no. 2001036MT

Dear Mr. Carson,

Thank you for your letter of 2nd July regarding our order. We are sorry to hear about your difficulties and hope those problems have been solved. We are happy to proceed with the order and would be grateful if you could send confirmation of the new delivery date.

We would also like to know whether it is possible to add a further two motors (catalogue no. 2203E) to the order.

We would like to take advantage of your offer concerning the discounted extended warranty. Could you please enclose the agreement with the delivery?

Could you please amend the invoice in accordance with these changes and send it to us?

I look forward to hearing from you soon.

Yours sincerely,
Jenny

Text B

Comprehension tasks

Task 1

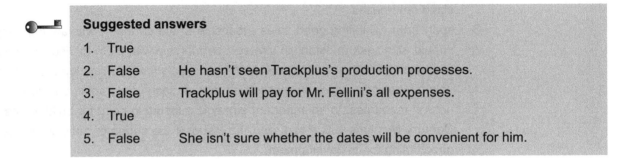

Suggested answers

1. c   2. d

Task 2

Suggested answers

1. True
2. False   He hasn't seen Trackplus's production processes.
3. False   Trackplus will pay for Mr. Fellini's all expenses.
4. True
5. False   She isn't sure whether the dates will be convenient for him.

Vocabulary

Task 3

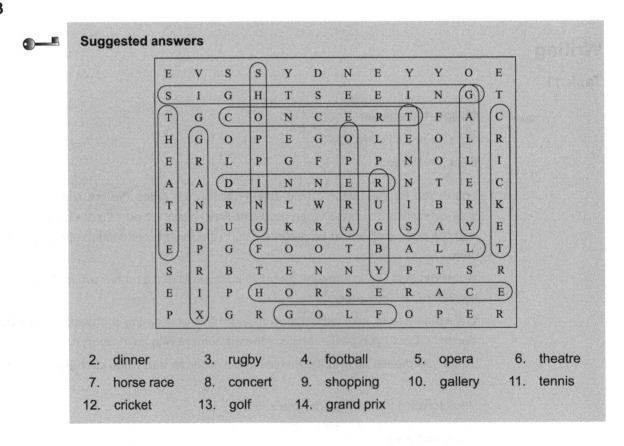

Suggested answers

2. dinner   3. rugby   4. football   5. opera   6. theatre
7. horse race   8. concert   9. shopping   10. gallery   11. tennis
12. cricket   13. golf   14. grand prix

Task 4

> **Suggested answers**
> 1. meet 2. finalise 3. place 4. build 5. set

Task 5

> **Suggested answers**
> 2. colleagues 3. satisfaction 4. inconvenience 5. valued customer
> 6. substantial 7. after-sales service 8. value for money

Speaking

Task 6

> **Suggested answers**
> - Not being polite, hospital, considerate or respectful, leaving a bad impression on clients.
> - Fail to take cultural or individual differences into consideration, such as client's personal taste or tattoos.
> - Send staff to corporate events without telling them why they are there or what they should do.
> - Be afraid of mentioning the business at corporate events.
> - Poor timing to bring up the matter of business at a social event.

Task 7 Ss may first discuss some popular ways to accommodate or entertain guests at home and abroad. Then they may refer their discussion to those appropriate events of entertaining business clients. Ss may summarise those important factors that make a corporate event successful.

Business communication

Task 8

> **Suggested answers**
> 1.
> - Hotel price and cost for accommodation should be within the budget.
> - Location should be as convenient as possible.
>
> 2.
> - Customs and business etiquette should be considered.
> - Itinerary should be in place, in details and in advance.

3.
- Budget should be made carefully.
- Reimbursement system should be incorporated into company policies.

Translation

Task 9

Suggested answers

1. 我很高兴在上周的米兰贸易展销会上终于见到了您。喜闻贵方对我们的"特拉克普拉斯系列产品"和青少年时尚运动服装及运动装备颇感兴趣，我们不胜感激。
2. 我们诚挚地邀请您在英国逗留几天，参观一下我们在牛津的工厂，以便您对我们的设备和生产工艺有一个大致的了解。
3. 至于日期，我们想是否可以定在本月末的哪一天。
4. 在一次讲话中，习总书记强调，为了将我国的对外开放水平提升到一个新的高度，"一带一路"倡议（包括丝绸之路经济带和21世纪海上丝绸之路）应该得到加强。
5. 生产率是指经济活动中产品或者服务被生产出来的效率，一般以每小时的产量或者单个工人的产量来计算。

Task 10

Suggested answers

1. There is a slight increase in the number of the purchasing agents compared with that of last year at this Guangzhou Fair, and the purchasers focus more on the new products with more advanced technology and more additional value.
2. This company manufactures and exports earphones, mobiles and computer accessories, which are extremely popular among the youngsters for their competitive prices in some countries.
3. Who is to steer the wheel with an overview to lead the company on the right path if you only have your head down doing everything from sales and marketing to accounting?
4. Different from private products, public facilities should be used fairly by users regardless of gender, age, cultural background and education.
5. We really appreciate this great friendship and from now on, we will be at your disposal anytime.

Writing

Task 11 Ss write a letter of acceptance of 120-140 words. It should be clear, appropriately formal and include all the five listed points. Ss should first work through the list of tips before writing their letters. If time is short, Ss write the letter for homework. If there is time for the writing task in class, Ss exchange letters and give each other feedback.

Suggested answer

Dear Ms Goddard,

With reference to your letter of 3 November, I am writing to thank you for your kind invitation.

I would be very pleased to accept your invitation to visit Oxford and see Trackplus's production facilities. I would also be interested in meeting your colleagues at Head Office, the design team in particular. I should also be delighted to accept your offer of arranging for me to see a play in the West End.

Unfortunately, due to a business trip abroad, I am unable to come to England at the end of November as you suggested. However, as I feel it is important that we meet before Christmas, I would be grateful if you could tell me if the second week of December would be suitable for you?

I look forward to hearing from you again.

Yours sincerely,
Paolo Fellini

Unit 3 Public relations

Objectives

To enable Ss to learn and talk about PR
To practise reading for specific information
To practise listening for specific information
To practise writing a formal letter of invitation
To enable Ss to describe the duties and responsibilities which jobs can entail

Essential vocabulary

Marketing and public relations	General
advertising campaign	to build (long-term relationships)
buzz	to deal with (the press)
commercial	dealership
PR (public relations)	emerging markets
press packs	to enter a competition
to rebrand	innovative
selling point	itineraries
social media	to maintain goodwill
strapline	public awareness
target audience	reputation
teaser campaign	venue
trade magazines	
viral (campaign)	
write-ups	

Warming up

Task 1 Ss read the list of duties and say whether they are the responsibilities of the PR Department.

> **Suggested answer**
> - communication with the press
> - public awareness of company values
> - development of the company's reputation

Task 2 Ss make a presentation based on the discussion Ss have just made in Task 1. Ss should set priorities for the responsibilities. Ss can also talk about what jobs PR managers do to fulfill those responsibilities.

Text A

Comprehension tasks

Task 1

Suggested answers
1. d   2. b

Task 2

Suggested answers
1. To plan and manage the public relations strategy and create a positive image of the company by providing information, dealing with the media, communicating with the public and personnel, and creating understanding with the public.
2. While PR Department is for communication with the press, public awareness of company values and development of the company's reputation, Marketing Department is for research into the public's needs, brand development and decisions about product pricing.
3. Communication skills, interpersonal skills, knowledge of the product and so on.
4. PR Department is very important to a company in the sense that it helps with receiving and providing information, establishing and maintaining a good relationship with the public, and thus, ensuring a long-term sustainable development of the company.

Vocabulary

Task 3

Suggested answers

verb	noun	adjective
persuade	persuasion	persuasive
support	support/supporter	supportive
diversify	diversification	diversified
rely (on)	reliability	reliable
entertain	entertainment	entertaining
encourage	encouragement	encouraging
compete	competition/competitor	competitive
grow	growth	growing

Task 4

Suggested answers
1. b   2. a   3. c   4. b   5. b   6. c   7. a   8. b

Task 5

Suggested answers
2. power
3. admit
4. issue
5. conditions
6. customers
7. policy
8. insurance
9. companies
10. concerns

Listening

Task 6 T asks Ss briefly to suggest how Škoda has managed to change its image since the early days of the brand (advertising campaign, PR innovative products, etc.). T then asks Ss to suggest what companies might do when launching a new ad campaign and how they might work at their image. Ss listen and check answers. Check Ss understand that The League Table is a list of the top cars in the U.K. as seen from the perspective of buyers. Ss listen to see if they were correct in their suggestions.

Suggested answer

Škoda launched an ad campaign with the slogan "It's a Škoda, honest" in 2000 because they recognised that there was a problem with their image and they wanted to change it. In addition, in 2006 they went to the Paris Automobile Show to launch the Joyster. They used the strapline "Made of Meaner Stuff" and created press and social media interest prior to the launch in order to get the message across to their target audience.

Audioscripts

Journalist	It's clear that Škoda's reputation has changed enormously over the last 20 years.
Catherine	Yes, yes it has. There has been a tremendous change. And you can see the results in the number of cars we are selling worldwide. You can also see it in the awards we're winning both as a company and for the cars we're producing. We recently won a number of prizes in the U.K. like "Best Manufacturer", the "Driver Power Award", and the "Overall Most Satisfying Brand".
Journalist	Yes. I was very impressed by your award for "Overall Most Satisfying Brand". You came top of the league table of most popular car-makers in the U.K. and beat Germany's Porsche and Japan's Lexus! And four of your models came in the top ten. That is amazing.
Catherine	Yes, we are very happy about that.

Journalist	I can imagine. So in 2011 the Škoda was voted as the most satisfying car to own in Britain. And now Škoda is one of the fastest growing car brands in the U.K. But it wasn't always like that.
Catherine	No, no it wasn't. When Škoda first launched in the U.K., people said they would rather buy anything than a Škoda.
Journalist	So what did the PR Department do to change the image?
Catherine	A number of things. In 2000 the company launched an ad campaign with the slogan. "It's a Škoda, honest". The idea was to change people's image of the company.
Journalist	That was a very brave thing to do.
Catherine	Yes, it was. The company recognised the problem and decided to fight it. It could have been a disaster, a complete disaster, but it worked.
Journalist	Yes, advertising can be very powerful.

Task 7

Suggested answers

1. c   2. b   3. a   4. c
5. c   6. b   7. a   8. a

Business communication

Task 8 In pairs Ss ask their partner what type of duties and responsibilities he or she would expect to have in a job. T may wish to note down common errors on the board for Ss to correct themselves after the activity.

Translation

Task 9

Suggested answers

1. 这意味着我负责与报纸、电视台和广播台打交道，同时还要负责与公众和英国的特译经销商沟通。
2. 另一方面，公共关系部更加注重建立和保持公司与公众之间的良好关系和相互理解。
3. 在公关部工作，你要与记者建立长期的关系，因为你会经常与他们打交道，而且信任至关重要。
4. 如果你能从你的国家或者地区需要什么人才的角度出发来理解广泛的全球模式，你就能先对手一步，并建立更强大的员工队伍。
5. 尽管瑞典的商科学生更倾向于选择大公司赚更多钱，但是他们的期望值差距并不大，只有4%多一点。

Task 10

Suggested answers

1. If you are one member of the Chinese enterprises conducting overseas communications, you may as well open your company's official website to see whether you have an English web page, whether the information on this English web page is complete, and whether the English expressions are technical and accurate enough or not.
2. The leading smart-phone companies possess a strong market position, a wide brand recognition, a stable supply chain and a mature channel of distribution. New market players are unlikely to compete with them and obtain huge market shares.
3. It should be the concern for many companies how to reasonably distribute the investment in product R&D and the service system, how to maintain the positive brand image in the service links and how to ensure smooth information transmission about the products.
4. There already exists the problem of interest imbalance among the manufacturers behind the market boom. The manufacturers firmly control all the dealership's links from new car sales to after-sales services, with interest balancing constantly in favor of the manufacturers.
5. Coordination and communication with the local tax, customs and other departments should be strengthened to set up a smooth working mechanism, and information should be reported on a regular basis to realise information sharing.

Writing

Task 11

Suggested answer

Dear Sir or Madam,

Hello, I am Smith Nick, director from PR Department of West End Electronic Company.

We are celebrating the opening of an international kindergarten fully sponsored by our company. Approximately 20 representatives from media are expected to attend this opening ceremony on Friday 29 October 2019. Honorable guests and community leaders will be invited to make speeches to audience.

As you have been with our company for at least 10 years, we are pleased to invite you to attend this opening ceremony. This special function will take place from 18:00 to 21:00 at Oriental Hotel, West Street, London. Cocktails and a buffet dinner will be provided. All participants will also be gifted with a souvenir.

With your participation, we are more confident in making more contributions to the local prosperity.

Please let me know whether you will be attending by returning the tear-off portion before 31 August.

> We hope you will be able to join us.
>
> Yours sincerely,
> Smith Nick
>
> ··
>
> Please return to Mrs. Hu, Administration Manager, before 31 August.
> I shall/shall not be attending the opening ceremony on Friday 29 October.
> Name..
> Designation..
> Signature..
> Date...

Text B

Comprehension tasks

Task 1

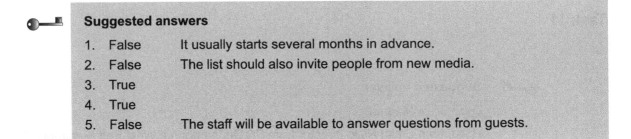

Suggested answers
1. b   2. b

Task 2

Suggested answers
1. False   It usually starts several months in advance.
2. False   The list should also invite people from new media.
3. True
4. True
5. False   The staff will be available to answer questions from guests.

Vocabulary

Task 3

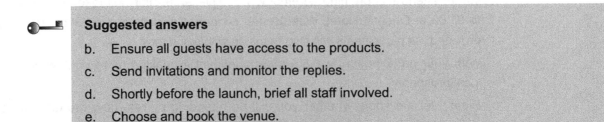

Suggested answers
b. Ensure all guests have access to the products.
c. Send invitations and monitor the replies.
d. Shortly before the launch, brief all staff involved.
e. Choose and book the venue.
f. Check everything and finalise the details.

Task 4

Suggested answers
2. withheld funding
3. comply with policies
4. bring about change
5. run a business
6. stretched their brand
7. carry product lines
8. provide healthcare
9. cling to ideals
10. creating loyalty

Task 5

Suggested answers
1. c 2. c 3. d 4. a 5. b 6. b 7. c 8. a
9. a 10. d 11. c 12. b 13. a 14. c 15. d 16. b

Speaking

Task 6 Ss discuss appropriate media through which the kindergarten can be publicised. T encourages Ss to provide further details of advantages and disadvantages of each type of media.

Task 7 T helps Ss brainstorm key factors in building a positive public image, which may be derived from its corporate culture, products and service, environmental consideration, the leader's reputation, charity contribution, fringe benefits and so on.

Business communication

Task 8 Ss should first agree on a certain type of products to promote. Then, based on the product's features and properties, Ss discuss the details of the launching event. If possible, Ss justify their choices as much as possible.

Translation

Task 9

Suggested answers
1. 要确保发行日不与其他制造商的日期相冲突。
2. 确定一下邀请名单（目标是最重要的汽车杂志、全国性报刊、主要的地方报纸和自由记者）。

3. 确认与现场相关的所有细节（客房预订、现场报告、菜单、停车场等），然后给嘉宾准备欢迎信息和日程安排。
4. 根据优信咨询在全球 12 个主要经济体的学生中所进行的一项调查，这个名单上的企业都是被学生们列为最富有吸引力排名前 100 的企业。
5. 绝大多数公司都是根据客户位置、原材料来源、劳动力供给、电力或水力供应及社区环境等重要因素来选址。

Task 10

Suggested answers

1. Freelance, like every other profession, is not suitable for everybody, even one with good literacy.
2. I took a short rest in the hotel's lobby, and asked for information about the train ticket to Dunhuang, Gansu Province, which was the next and also the most important stop on my itinerary.
3. On our part we wish to finalise this lengthy negotiation by overcoming all difficulties and come to a win-win result on the basis of mutual respect for the basic interests of both parties.
4. From the perspective of marketing, a new product, after being launched, will experience different development stages and the pricing policies at different stages will also be different.
5. Every country has its own commercial laws and regulations. To establish a long-term brand and to obtain a goodwill, one must obey the host country's commercial laws and regulations, particularly those that clash with those in one's own country.

Writing

Task 11 Ss write a letter of acceptance of 120-140 words. It should be clear, appropriately formal and include all the five listed points. Ss should first work through the list of tips before writing their letters. If time is short, Ss write the letter for homework. If there is time for the writing task in class, Ss exchange letters and give each other feedback.

Suggested answer

Dear Sir/Madam,

I am pleased to be able to invite you to the launch of *English Tomorrow*, the exciting new multi-level CD-ROM programme for business English learners. *English Tomorrow* is published by Talk International in co-operation with Bookers Publishers.

The official launch will take place at 3:00 p.m. on 25 July at the Royal Bell Hotel, South Harford, Somerset.

During the afternoon there will be an opportunity for you to try out the material. Moreover, the designers—Mark Brightman and Sally Waters, and representatives of Bookers Publishers will be present to answer any questions you may have.

I hope your schedule will allow you to accept our invitation. I would be grateful if you could confirm your attendance by Saturday 20 June at the latest and look forward to hearing from you.

Yours sincerely,
Ruth Williams
PR Manager

Unit 4 Ordering goods

Objectives

To enable Ss to talk about making and changing orders
To raise awareness of clarity in writing
To practise writing short emails
To enable Ss to negotiate order change

Essential vocabulary

Suppliers	Catalogues	General
article	catalogue	headquarters
buyer	collection	to knit
to cancel (an order)	length	to reduce
cancellation	measurement	skirt
to confirm (an order)	to shorten	
confirmation	standard	
delivery	to standardise	
goods		
mail order		
to order		
piece		
quantity		
to recommend		
stock		
to supply		
supplier		

Warming up

Task 1   Ss brainstorm as many ways as possible of placing an order of goods (via sending emails, making phone calls, signing contracts, etc.).

Task 2   Ss brainstorm the important issues when placing an order (say, competitive price, high quality, on-time delivery, satisfactory after-sale service, negotiation of order change, etc.).

Text A

Comprehension tasks

Task 1

Suggested answers

1. False — The products are women's skirts.
2. True
3. False — He wants to order the skirts in a standard length only.
4. False — She wants to decrease the order quantity by 400 pieces.
5. True

Task 2 Ss read Antonella's reply to Korinna and answer the questions.

Suggested answers

1. To query Korinna's change of order.
2. Antonella thought the two different lengths for each skirt had been agreed when Mr. Hubner was in Italy.
3. Antonella is going to wait for Korinna to confirm the information about the length of skirts required before contacting the vendors.

Vocabulary

Task 3

Suggested answers

1. recommended
2. finalise
3. suppliers
4. standardise

Task 4

Suggested answers

1. places
2. delivers
3. produces
4. arrive
5. issues
6. orders
7. receives

Task 5

Suggested answers

deliver goods   fill in a delivery note   pay import duty
ship a consignment   negotiate with the supplier

1. deliver goods	2. fill in a delivery note	3. pay import duty
4. ship a consignment	5. negotiate with the supplier	

Listening

Task 6 Ss listen to the telephone conversation to find out what Antonella has to do.

Suggested answer

She has to call Cristi and Faci to confirm the order for 400 standard length skirts before emailing Korinna to let her know.

Audioscripts

Antonella	Pronto, Zanetti.
Korinna	Hello? Antonella?
Antonella	Yes?
Korinna	Hello. It's Korinna Krämer from Schneider in Hamburg.
Antonella	Oh, hi Korinna. How are you?
Korinna	Fine, thanks. I'm ringing about the skirts for the summer catalogue.
Antonella	Oh yes. The Cristi and Faci skirts. Did you speak to Mr. Hubner?
Korinna	Yes, I did. We definitely want only the standard length.
Antonella	OK. So that's the Cristi and Faci in standard length only. Right.
Korinna	And have you spoken to the vendors about quantity yet?
Antonella	No, not yet. I thought I'd wait until we knew what was happening about the lengths.
Korinna	Do you think you could speak to them soon, though? We don't have much time left before the deadline.
Antonella	No problem. I'll contact them this morning. And is it still only 400 pieces of each?
Korinna	Yes, that's right.
Antonella	OK. I'll email you as soon as I've spoken to them.
Korinna	That's great, Antonella. Thanks for your help.
Antonella	That's OK. You'll be hearing from me later.
Korinna	Great. I'll expect your email then. Bye.

Task 7 T asks Ss to read the six functions listed. Ss listen again more carefully to phrases used to express the functions. T then asks Ss to think of other possible spoken phrases for the same functions.

Suggested answers

1. I'm ringing about...
2. We definitely want... / So that's...
3. Do you think you could...?

> 4. I'll call them...
> 5. Thanks for...
> 6. I'll email you...You'll be hearing from me later.

T then asks Ss if they can suggest formal written equivalents. Ss can be encouraged to keep lists off normal written phrases and less formal spoken ones as they will need them for the exam.

> **Suggested answers**
> 1. I would like to (inform you/request, etc.) ...
> 2. I am writing to confirm that...
> 3. Could you please...? I would be grateful if you could...
> 4. I will / I shall...
> 5. Thank you for / I am very grateful for...
> 6. I look forward to (hearing from you / seeing you, etc.)

Business communication

Task 8 T asks Ss to brainstorm the usual procedures to change an original order (confirming the original order, stating the difficulties from the buyer's side or mentioning the problems of samples, negotiating a change or cancelling the order, etc.).

Translation

Task 9

> **Suggested answers**
> 1. 哈布纳先生和其他买家已经完成了夏装系列的分析报告和推荐计划。
> 2. 法西公司的裙子在底部有个开口,这样不利于顾客调整裙子的长度,所以我们同意卖家提供两种长度的裙子。
> 3. 至于减少订单产品的总量,我得和卖家确认了裙子长度等信息之后才能回复您。
> 4. 这些(医疗保健)组织正在拓展和检验不同的方法,从而增进协作,使得医疗保健标准化和高效化,确保医疗保健一直处于高水准。
> 5. 我们很遗憾地通知你们,贵公司发来的产品比我们当初下单时看到的样品质量差得多。

Task 10

> **Suggested answers**
> 1. Five workers from companies in sectors such as television repair, delivery business and public service have been robbed at gunpoint in the city since February 20.

2. Several famous stock market specialists clearly pointed out that the stock market was reacting considerably to some big economic events.
3. Some middle-level management personnel have noticed that some data in the annual report are not accurate or consistent, such as the calculation of purchase volume of local families.
4. The condition for the localisation of automation application technology has not emerged in China, so currently goods stowing by machines is instead less efficient than by human labour, for the standard stowage cannot be realised yet.
5. I have read the catalogue and brochures you attached in your letter and known a little about the export products of your company, but we still need to negotiate more to facilitate mutual understanding.

Writing

Task 11 Ss compose a reply to Antonella's email. It should be concise (40-50 words) and should contain all three points listed. Functional expressions from the unit should be used where appropriate. If time is short, Ss do the writing task for homework. If Ss do the writing in class, they work individually or in pairs then present their draft to each other and offer feedback.

> **Suggested answer**
>
> Dear Antonella,
>
> Thank you for your email. In answer to your queries, I can confirm that the measurement charts do not need changing and all knitted skirts will now be produced in a standard length.
>
> We would like to propose a delivery date of 30 June. Does that suit you?
>
> Best regards,
> Korinna

Text B

Comprehension tasks

Task 1

> **Suggested answers**
>
> 1. c   2. c

Task 2

> **Suggested answer**
>
> 6-5-7-3-1-4-2

Unit 4   Ordering goods   35

Vocabulary

Task 3 Ss match each function with two phrases, one from a telephone conversation and one from a letter. T elicits other written phrases Ss know in each category; they will be very useful in the Writing Test. As conciseness is important in the Writing Test, T makes sure that Ss know short written ways of fulfilling these functions, e.g. Requesting: Please..., Giving information: Please note that... .

Suggested answers

		Telephone	Letter
1.	Referring to a letter	I got your letter about...	Further to your letter of...
2.	Suggesting	Why don't we...?	We propose...
3.	Giving information	Here's the information you wanted.	I trust you will find the following points of interest.
4.	Asking for confirmation	Let me know when you have a definite date.	Could you please confirm the confirmation date?
5.	Asking for information	Can you send me details on...?	I would be very grateful if you could send me...
6.	Reminding	Don't forget that...	May I remind you that...?

Task 4

Suggested answers

1. in   2. by   3. in   4. to   5. at

Task 5

Suggested answers

(1) confirmed   (2) articles   (3) reduce   (4) need   (5) regards

Speaking

Task 6 T introduces the idea of mail-order companies. T asks Ss what qualities these companies may look for in their suppliers (attractive price, reliability, consistent quality, flexibility, just-in-time delivery policy, etc.).

Task 7 T asks Ss to brainstorm the common problems emerging in the course of placing orders (negotiation of prices, change of quantity of goods, difference between samples and delivered goods, deliver means, buyers' dissatisfaction, etc.).

Business communication

Task 8 T asks Ss to brainstorm the common reasons for the change of orders in several industries, for example, clothing, foods, cosmetics. In the industry of clothing, the material, the color, the style, the length, etc. will likely contribute to change of orders. In foods industry, the issue of healthiness, fat containing, protein containing, etc. may cause the change of orders. In cosmetics industry, protection of skins, price, user-friendliness, etc. will be crucial.

Translation

Task 9

Suggested answers

1. 作为公司结构调整的一部分，接下来的采购目录必须大规模削减。
2. 然而，我方可以确认的是我方仍然保留原订单中将于 8 月 22 日发货的斯嘉丽裙装。
3. 对于我方改变订单给贵方带来的不便我深表歉意，期待以后继续和贵方合作。
4. 古铁雷斯 1 月 10 日说他不会参加特朗普的就职典礼，但会参加之后一天的大规模抗议游行。
5. 作为重组州政府和改进顾客服务的重拳之一，专门小组提出了 187 条议案，涉及 200 条相关规定，而且州长打算将其全部付诸实施。

Task 10

Suggested answers

1. The following is the full text of an action plan on the China-proposed Belt and Road Initiative proposed by the National Development and Reform Commission, the Ministry of Foreign Affairs, and the Ministry of Commerce of the People's Republic of China, with the State Council's authorisation.
2. Many young people have witnessed the glamor of Internet enterprises and instantaneously intended to start a business, only to find that they could not undergo the difficulties and then prepare to quit.
3. A lot of local and foreign websites do not have forthcoming methods to protect users from hackers who exploit weaknesses in the servers.
4. It's natural for students to change their minds as they go through college—but to tell them they are just not good enough to achieve their dreams is never acceptable.
5. At a certain point, the potential inconvenience of cash may force people into utilising other forms of payment that may not be as secure.

Writing

Task 11

Suggested answer

Report on Stanton, Inc. 2011

Introduction
This report aims to assess the 2011 balance sheet of Stanton, Inc. and make a recommendation regarding whether we should invest in Stanton's shares.

Findings

Stanton seems to have had difficulties in selling its products in 2011. This could have been due to difficult trading conditions or ageing and unpopular products. Furthermore, the increase in money owed by debtors suggests that customers are also having difficulties.

Stanton has also increased its won debt to the banks, yet little of this has been invested in new plant and machinery for the future.

Conclusion

Stanton has had a difficult year and now has surplus stock, cash flow problems and substantially increased debt.

Recommendation

It is recommended that we do not invest in Stanton at the present but review the situation in six months' time.

Review Test 1

Part I Listening comprehension

Task 1

> **Suggested answers**
> (1) training course
> (2) Managing People
> (3) 13(th) August / August 13(th)
> (4) Virginia Little

Audioscripts

Joanna	Joanna Rivers.
Peter	Hello, Joanna. It's Peter. Is David there?
Joanna	No, I'm sorry, Peter. He's just left the office.
Peter	What time will he be back?
Joanna	Not till tomorrow, I'm afraid. Can I take a message?
Peter	Yes, OK. It's about a training course he was interested in. Let me see, he asked about Financing Start-ups but he decided on Managing People. We first planned it for July but we've moved it to 13 August.
Joanna	So that was Managing People and it's now in August?
Peter	Yes, so he'll have to be quick if he's interested. Carol Smith who usually runs it can't do it this time so he'll have to call Virginia Little directly and talk to her about taking part. Her number's 01723 887762.
Joanna	OK, Peter. I'll make sure he gets this when he comes in.
Peter	OK, and one other thing. Tell David to mention my name. Virginia's an old friend of mine.

Task 2

> **Suggested answers**
> 1. b   2. g   3. f   4. e   5. c

Audioscripts

1. Well, it's not used that often in the office except for meetings and presentations in the conference room. But sometimes when you do need it, you can't find it, because one of the managers takes it home sometimes. I think he uses it partially to watch films but also to make sure his presentations look exactly the way he wants them to.

2. We recently got a new one that's got hundreds of functions on it. It can sort and staple and do all sorts of other clever things. Of course, not all of us know how to use all these functions so even if we want to do something simple like copy a document on two sides we have to find someone to help. But it's really great and much faster than our old one was.

3. It's really helpful when I have to be out of the office for a while. If I don't answer my line after three rings, everything gets transferred automatically. And when I arrive in the morning I can check to see if there are any messages. Because our offices are all over the world, people get in touch when they have time. I don't like to take it home with me because I often forget to switch if off and I don't want to mix work and my private life. But it's great because sometimes people just send a short text message and sometimes they call and explain exactly what they need.

4. Whenever I tell people that we have one in the office, they're always very impressed. They think the company must do some kind of important, secret business. The truth is our Dispatch Department uses it, not our main office. They collect all the waste paper from the photocopier and printer and use it for packaging.

5. It's been pretty much replaced by email, but I still use it now and then. If I want to send a signed document to someone or a quick drawing, then it's the best solution. It's quick, easy to use and you don't have to worry about compatibility either. And once or twice it's been a life-saver when the photocopier's broken down.

Task 3

Suggested answers

| 1. a | 2. c | 3. a | 4. b |
| 5. a | 6. c | 7. b | 8. a |

Audioscripts

Alex Job losses are expected at the Manchester plant of the beauty products manufacturer, Vie Vitale. Sophie Jones has been following the story and is in our Manchester studio. Good morning, Sophie.

Sophie Good morning, Alex.

Alex So, job losses, Sophie? How are things going? We've been hearing reports of up to 300 jobs going.

Sophie Well, if Vie Vitale does go ahead with restructuring and that includes the disposal of its manufacturing base, then as many as 200 of the 500 jobs here are far from guaranteed.

Alex And where exactly will these cuts be made, Sophie?

Sophie Well, most would almost certainly be in the manufacturing division. This is an area Vie Vitale wants to get out of completely. And if this happens, then it would have serious consequences for jobs in distribution. However, the company wants to focus on its product development, so there's unlikely to be any losses there. At least, that's what the company's saying this morning.

Alex	So very little good news there. But why should the company suddenly find itself in such a difficult position?
Sophie	Well, the health and beauty retail sector is still as fashionable as ever and has attracted a lot of new companies to the market. The sad truth is, though, that these new companies now have equally good if not better ideas at the same kind of price. And I think this is the fundamental problem. And last year, La Face, the French manufacturer, brought out a new range—again, very similar types of products, very similar sorts of ideas.
Alex	So how well are La Face doing?
Sophie	Well, actually, they haven't been doing that well either. In fact, only last week they announced they're no longer going to focus on their own retail outlets, but rather on the mail order side of the business instead. They're also considering selling through department stores, but nothing's been confirmed yet. So Vie Vitale isn't alone in feeling incredible pressure.
Alex	Well, it sounds like the problem they're all having is that it's getting quite crowded. So what does all this mean for Vie Vitale's share price?
Sophie	Well, if we look at the share price over the last year, you can see that although it started high at the beginning of the year and looked steady in the first six months, there's been a huge drop since then, reaching its lowest point last week where the City really lost confidence in what they were doing.
Alex	Right. Now, Vie Vitale's corporate image used to be unique, didn't it? So how are they planning to establish themselves as the market leader once more?
Sophie	Well, Alex, they're not giving away too many details just yet, but it seems they're intending to freshen up their shops and update their corporate look. You know, all their packaging. There's certainly no news of any new product lines or any change in their basic values.
Alex	But what about the number of shops? Any change there, Sophie?
Sophie	Well, in fact, what they're doing is buying franchises back. They feel that if they're in control of their shops, they're in control of their corporate image. We've heard nothing about shop closures.
Alex	So how many of their shops do they now own?
Sophie	Well, they started the process a few months ago and they've now regained control of all their French outlets. And they should have ownership of all their German shops by early next year. As there are more outlets in the U.K., it'll take a bit longer here. I think the name of the game is definitely going to be control.

Part II Reading and writing

Task 4

Suggested answers

| 1. a | 2. c | 3. a | 4. b | 5. d | 6. c | 7. d | 8. b |
| 9. a | 10. c | 11. c | 12. a | 13. c | 14. c | 15. a | 16. d |

Task 5

Suggested answers

1. a 2. b 3. d 4. b 5. c 6. a 7. c

Task 6

Suggested answers

1. d 2. c 3. c 4. b 5. a

Task 7

Suggested answer

Dear colleagues,

This is an official reminder about the introduction of Guide, the new benefits policies provided in the company of IBM.

Given the current situation, the old benefits policies of our company are not effective to help motivate hardworking staff. Since last year, the administrative office has been working on some new policies and conditions under which benefits will be distributed more reasonably. Last week, the Guide has gained the approval of the Board meeting and will come into effect in the coming new year. Any regulation or procedure previously issued not consistent with this Guide will be superseded.

The Guide is the employee manual as well as the basic source of information relating to the benefits policies and programmes to all employees.

We strongly recommend that you read the Guide carefully and kindly archive it for future use. In case that you have an enquiry or further explanation about policies in the Guide, please contact us at Linda186@hotmail.com.

Please check the attachment for details.

Best regards,
Linda
Administrative secretary of IBM

Part III Business knowledge and translation

Task 8

Suggested answers

1. balance sheet
   Definition: A written statement of the amount of money and property that a company or a person has, including amounts of money that are owed or are owing, usually referring to the general financial state of a company.
   Translation: 资产负债表

2. enterprise

   Definition: An enterprise is a company or business. (It also means the activity of managing companies and businesses and starting new ones. Enterprise is the ability to think of new and effective things to do, together with an eagerness to do them.)

   Translation: 企业；创业；开创精神

3. intangible asset

   Definition: Assets that are saleable though not material or physical, for example, intellectual property, patent, reputation and financial credit.

   Translation: 无形资产

4. fringe benefit

   Definition: Fringe benefits are extra things that some people get from their job in addition to their salary, for example, a car, paid holidays or medical insurance.

   Translation: （附加）福利

5. human resource

   Definition: Human resources refer to the employed and to-be-employed people that staff and operate an organisation, as contrasted with the financial and material resources of an organisation. It also refers to the function of dealing with the people and issues such as compensation and benefits, recruiting and hiring employees, performance management, training, and so on.

   Translation: 人力资源

Task 9

Suggested answer

For Wal-Mart, the largest retailer in the United States, the days are tough. The retailer has long been accused of destroying small-town American life and being stingy in paying wages. Recently, the company was also strongly critisized for reducing the health insurance benefits of its workers.

Unit 5 Relocation

> **Objectives**
>
> To enable Ss to talk about relocation, office space and facilities
> To practise reading for gist
> To practise listening for directions
> To practise letter writing
> To review comparatives and language of similarity and difference

Essential vocabulary

Relocating	General
assistance	aim
barrier	brain power
to be made redundant	challenges
career move	career ladder
demand	to compare (favourably with...)
destination	to conclude
documentation	to search
expat (expatiate)	supervision
to fulfil (needs)	
immigration	
migrant	
shipping	
skills shortage	
to sponsor	
storage	
tradespeople	

Warming up

Task 1 In pairs Ss discuss why a person might relocate to another part of the same country (more or better job opportunities, better infrastructure, partner relocation, etc.) and to another country (career move, gain experience, family reasons, etc.). T then asks Ss briefly to predict why someone might wish to relocate to Australia in particular.

Text A

Comprehension tasks

Task 1

> **Suggested answers**
> 1. e 2. b 3. f 4. a 5. d

Task 2

> **Suggested answers**
> 1. b 2. b

Vocabulary

Task 3

> **Suggested answers**
> (1) predictions (2) supervision (3) demand (4) shortage
> (5) recruiting (6) barrier (7) sponsor

Task 4

> **Suggested answers**
> (1) assess (2) offers (3) arranges (4) conclude
> (5) fulfils (6) compare (7) recommend (8) is made / be made
> (9) have been approached

Task 5

> **Suggested answers**
>
> **Infrastructure**
> motorways, public transport, road access, waterways, airports
>
> **Cost factors**
> grants, renovation costs, running costs, rent
>
> **Labour market**
> skills, availability of workers, employment law, local wage levels

Listening

Task 6 Ss listen to Gerald Slater giving directions to an office site and mark the correct site (A-J) on the map. T should clearly indicate the starting point before Ss listen. Ss are then asked to read the audioscript to pinpoint the language Jim uses to make sure he has the correct information.

Suggested answers

The correct site is **C**.

Jim repeats Gerald's instructions to make sure he understood them.

Gerald gives names for the streets and describes what Jim will see so that he knows that he is going in the right direction.

Audioscripts

Gerald	PLP Immobilier. Bonjour?
Jim	Hello, Gerald? It's Jim Flower here.
Gerald	Hello, Jim. Nice to hear from you. What can I do for you?
Jim	Listen, Gerald. I'm just on my way to have a look at that office site you mentioned the other day.
Gerald	Oh, yeah?
Jim	The thing is, I know the street name, but I can't remember where it is exactly. Do you think you could give me directions?
Gerald	Yes, of course. Where are you now?
Jim	Well, I've just parked the car and I'm in rue de Tournelles just outside a supermarket.
Gerald	Rue de Tournelles? Oh, yes. I know. Now let me see. OK. Right. Now, if you look right, you'll see a bank on the corner. It's called BNP.
Jim	OK. Yes, I can see that.
Gerald	Right. Well, walk to the bank, to the corner, and that's rue de Balzac. You turn left there and cross over to the other side of the street.
Jim	So I am on my way to the bank and then I turn left at the corner and cross the street?
Gerald	That's right. Then take the first road on the right. That's rue de Paradis. Oh, and you'll see a big café on that corner. Keep going along that street until you come to a theatre. I think you'll cross over two or three other streets on the way, but just keep straight on till you reach the theatre.
Jim	Right, OK. So, I take the first right and just keep going straight on until the theatre.
Gerald	That's right. Now just before the theatre, on the left, is a small street. You go down there, and about halfway along is a kind of a square, with a statue in the middle.
Jim	That was a square with a statue?
Gerald	Yes, and the building is on the right. It's a large, white, modern-looking building. You can't miss it.
Jim	Thanks, Gerald. I'll be in touch soon.
Gerald	Bye, Jim. Oh, and send me a quick email to let me know what you think of it.

Unit 5 Relocation

Task 7 Ss listen again and work in pairs and take turns in giving each other directions to and from places on the map.

Business communication

Task 8 T asks Ss to brainstorm the preparations for relocating in a developed English-speaking country for career development after graduation, for example, a plan to improve English, especially listening and speaking; to familiarize with the culture, customs and the economic and social situation of the target country; to enrich the knowledge and techniques in the target industry, etc.

Translation

Task 9

Suggested answers

1. 员工可能会担心自己在当前工作的公司成为一个多余的人。
2. 公司有时会增设海外分公司，很多员工会把此当作职业晋升的良机，进而提升自己在公司的受关注度。
3. （政府的移民打分制度）优先考虑那些乐于花钱提升员工的雇主，打分依据他们的英语技能、工作经历、卓越资历和年龄等因素。
4. 为满足占GDP总量高达70%的国内消费，美国有着巨大的进口需求。
5. 公司的人力资源部经理向工人提供了有关新移民政策的相关信息，但与此同时也肯定了保持其员工组成多样性的必要。

Task 10

Suggested answers

1. In order to guarantee the health of children and teenagers, the government plans to propose to prohibit producing, publicising, promoting and sponsoring electronic and other new-style cigarettes.
2. The deeds of your company will directly influence thousands of our partners and suppliers on fulfilling their duties and responsibilities.
3. It is extremely crucial to reinforce government's supervision on banking and insurance industries for the stability and prosperity of the finance market and the maintenance of good and steady economic operation.
4. Experts attending the conference maintain that challenges confronted in economic transformation are no fewer than those in economic crises.
5. There still exists a belief that the brain power of the board of directors is enough to tackle the severe challenges the company is currently confronted with.

Writing

Task 11 Ss compose a 120-140 word letter to Gerard requesting further information. It should be clear and appropriate. It should also contain all the five points highlighted in the handwritten notes. T may wish to set the letter for homework. However, if Ss write the letter in class, T could ask Ss to exchange letters and give each other feedback.

> **Suggested answer**
>
> Dear Gerald,
>
> I am writing to say that after visiting the site, my company is very interested in renting the office premises at 4 place Jean Moulin. However, I would be very grateful if you could give me some further information.
>
> Firstly, would it be possible for you to tell me which companies share the site? Could you also tell me how many floors there are in the building in total? We are only interested in renting a single floor of the building. Would this be possible? We also need natural light in the office. Is it available?
>
> You say the property is near two metro stations. Can you tell me which ones they are?
>
> I would also like to know where the additional surface car-parking is exactly, and whether it has an extra cost.
>
> I look forward to hearing from you soon.
>
> Yours sincerely,
>
> xxx

Text B

Comprehension tasks

Task 1

> **Suggested answers**
> 1. b   2. b

Task 2

> **Suggested answers**
> 1. e   2. c   3. g   4. b

Vocabulary

Task 3

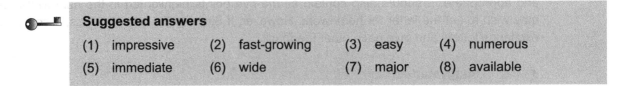

Suggested answers

(1) impressive (2) fast-growing (3) easy (4) numerous
(5) immediate (6) wide (7) major (8) available

Task 4

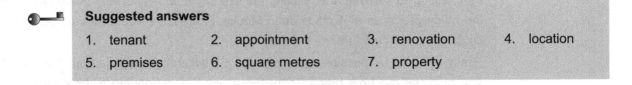

Suggested answers

1. tenant   2. appointment   3. renovation   4. location
5. premises   6. square metres   7. property

Task 5

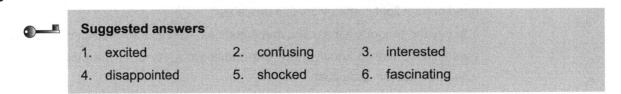

Suggested answers

1. excited   2. confusing   3. interested
4. disappointed   5. shocked   6. fascinating

Speaking

Task 6 Ss discuss in pairs what arrangements people have to make when relocating to another country (find accommodation, organise work permits, etc.), and what other things they might need to take into account if they're relocating alone or with family (e.g. organise schools, work for their partners, etc.).

Task 7 Ss brainstorm the respective merits and demerits of relocating in Australia and China.

Suggested answers

In Australia

Merits: higher salary; more holidays; excellent natural environment; court house…

Demerits: fewer people to communicate with; foreign culture…

In China

Merits: recognition of culture and customs; shared faith and values; more frequent social interactions…

Demerits: smaller salary; busy schedule; higher housing cost…

Business communication

Task 8 T asks Ss to brainstorm the respective merits and demerits of work in a first-tier city or another medium or small-size city. It depends on the balance of pursuing career development and guaranteeing an affordable living cost. T can encourage students of different types to maintain contradictory opinions.

Translation

Task 9

Suggested answers
1. 对于有些公司来说，公司形象局限于能被人识别的标识和被人记住的标语。
2. 最后这个（公司选址的）因素比它给人的第一印象更能够代表一个公司及其公司的理念。
3. 即使简陋的办公室与工厂相连一并坐落在一个不景气的工业园区的边缘，这也能体现公司的运营理念。
4. 2000 年，爱沙尼亚政府第一个宣布将人们获取上网的权利等同于获取食物和住所的权利一样，属于基本人权。
5. 对于亚马逊给顾客的购物体验带来的科技创新，我们只能想象。

Task 10

Suggested answers
1. The increase comes as more people gain access to mobile phones, so the popularity of mobile phone payment and Internet finance are developing at a fast speed.
2. The tea sold by our company is of high quality, diversified range and a high reputation at home and abroad.
3. The shrinking of recent markets leads to an obvious decrease of revenue in the new quarter. Therefore, we must strictly supervise product quality, develop product potential and explore new growth areas.
4. The premise of improving people's livelihood is to guarantee sufficient employment, which relies on vocational education cultivating vocational skilled talents on a large scale.
5. The institution announced that the event would not bring about immediate threats to people in other areas and that the residents in neighbouring areas of nuclear power plant had evacuated in advance.

Writing

Task 11 Report on location of the new assembly plant.

Suggested answer

Introduction

The purpose of this report is to assess the suitability of locating the new assembly plant in Hamburg, north Germany, and recommend a suitable site.

Findings

Hamburg has excellent transport links by sea, road, and air. It is one of Europe's busiest ports. Germany's two main motorways pass through the city and it has a fast-growing international airport. It is also a gateway to Scandinavia and central Europe with a fast rail link to Berlin.

The region has an educated and skilled workforce with a strong engineering tradition. It will be possible to source many components locally.

Recommendation

It is suggested that the fast-developing business park northwest of the city would be an ideal site because it is next to the motorway and 10 minutes from both the harbour and rail terminal. We recommend that the site should be studied in more details.

Unit 6 Work safety and rights

Objectives

To enable Ss to talk about safety and rights
To practise reading for gist and specific information
To practise listening for specific information
To review the language of obligation and prohibition

Essential vocabulary

Health and safety	
absent (from work)	painkillers
accident	(to take) precautions
cause for concern	to prevent
ergonomic	reasonable
findings	to require
first aid	repetitive strain injury
to handle	to review
to harm / to cause harm	to revise
to hurt	risk
incident	to slip
injury	stitches
law	to take into account
liability	to trip
to lift	workplace
to lose your balance	

Warming up

Task 1 T introduces the topic of safety and rights by asking Ss questions, for example, "Have you or one of your colleagues ever had an accident at work?", "What happened?", "Who is responsible for safety and rights at your workplace or school?", etc. T elicits from Ss what a safety and rights policy is. (In the U.K. every employee is legally obliged to prepare a written policy on health and safety which displays in the workplace outlining ways to deal with potential hazards.) T also elicits what training can be expected (In the U.K. each workplace has a nominated safety officer who checks the health and safety provision of the workplace and provides regular training to staff) and what happens when an accident occurs (Under the Occupational Safety and Health Act, a report must be made when illness or injury results in medical treatment, transfers to another job, restricted work or motion, or loss of consciousness). T could also point out that in the U.S. there is also an Occupational Safety and Health Administration and similar laws. Posters must be hung up in workplaces and specific records of accidents must be kept.

Ss work in pair and think of three possible accidents that can happen in an office (e.g. falling over computer cables, tripping over the carpet, injury caused by lifting heavy objects).

Task 2 Ss work in pairs and discuss the questions. Accidents happen mostly because of the lack of safety sense or imperfect safety facilities. Companies or school may prevent accidents by taking precautions, such as laying down safety regulations, nominating a safety officer, assessing safety risks, improving the workplace facilities, etc.

Text A

Comprehension tasks

Task 1

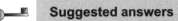

Suggested answers
1. b   2. a   3. e   4. d   5. c

Task 2

Suggested answers
1. True
2. True
3. True
4. False (Think about people who may not be in the workplace all the time, e.g. cleaners, contractors, maintenance personnel. Members of the public who visit your workplace should also be included. There is a chance that they could be hurt by your activities.)
5. False (First, ask yourself whether you have done all the things that the law says you have got to do. Then ask yourself whether generally-accepted industry standards are in place.)
6. False (In any case, it is good practice to review your assessment from time to time. Don't amend your assessment for every trivial change or each new job; but if a new job introduces significant new hazards of its own, you will want to consider them in their own right and do whatever you need to keep the risks down.)

Vocabulary

Task 3

Suggested answers
2. maternity leave
3. shop steward

4. wage packet
   5. disciplinary procedure
   6. sickness benefit
   7. hourly rate
   8. social security

Task 4

Suggested answers
   2. disciplinary
   3. time off
   4. absent
   5. time-keeping
   6. sue
   7. rights
   8. unfair dismissal
   9. notify
   10. ultimatum

Task 5

Suggested answers

1. a	2. c	3. c	4. a	5. b
6. c	7. a	8. c	9. d	10. c
11. a	12. b	13. b	14. a	15. d

Listening

Task 6

Suggested answers

1. b 2. f 3. a 4. e 5. g

Audioscripts

1. I didn't really feel I was abusing the system. I mean everybody does it. Just a few small things really—a fax here, a few photocopies there. I felt it was justified. After all, I did do a lot of unpaid overtime and I took work home with me. They seemed really pleased with my performance, so I honestly didn't think they'd mind.

2. My boss didn't mind if I arrived a couple of minutes late in the mornings but if I wanted to leave on time, well that was a completely different story. Well, after six months, I'd just had enough of it, working late every day of the week. So one day I told him straight: I'd only work the hours I'd agreed in my contract.

3. I was having problems because I just couldn't seem to prioritise my work and organise my time. So I suppose it looked to my boss as if I couldn't do the job. But it's ridiculous really. I could do it, but I just couldn't seem to keep up with the workload. And this was a place where results were everything.

4. I knew my turn would come soon. But I hated the whole idea of spending three hours in the car every day just getting to work and back. It was OK for some of the others, I mean, they lived nearer the new site. But if I'd had to work overtime, I'd never have got home before 9 o'clock. Well, in the end, I just couldn't do it. And I wouldn't do it. And that's what I told them.

5. I suppose they didn't want to carry me any longer. I think people just got fed up with having to cover for me and take on all my work when I was away. But it seems a pretty poor show to sack someone for something that isn't their fault. I mean, no-one wants to be ill, do they?

Task 7 T asks Ss to look at the accident report form. Before Ss listen to the recording, T asks them to predict the missing words in Part D. Ss then listen to the conversation between a company doctor and an employee.

Suggested answers
1. the factory   2. his balance   3. stitches   4. painkillers

Audioscripts

Doctor	That cut on your leg looks nasty. And you've got a bruise on your arm. How did it happen?
Peter	Well, I was in the factory and got a call on my mobile phone. It was really loud and I couldn't hear so I had to look for a quieter spot.
Doctor	Aren't you supposed to leave your phone in the office when you go to the factory?
Peter	Yes, usually. But I was expecting a really important call from a supplier about a part we needed and didn't want to miss the call so I took it with me.
Doctor	And then?
Peter	Well, I finished my call and walked back across the floor to the assembly line because I had to talk to some of the workers and my phone rang again.
Doctor	And what did you do?
Peter	I couldn't hear the person again and as this was the call I was waiting for I began to walk over to the quieter area again.
Doctor	So what happened? Did you trip over something?
Peter	No. I was talking to the supplier and suddenly a forklift ran into me. The driver was trying to get parts to the line for production and he was in a hurry. I didn't see him because I was concentrating on the call.
Doctor	And so you lost your balance and fell?

Peter	Yes, I landed on the floor but I was fine. In fact, I picked up my phone and just continued the call. But the production manager insisted that I come in and see you.
Doctor	You really must be more careful in the factory you know. If there is really a problem, the company doesn't have to take responsibility when you don't follow the rules. Do you feel sick or dizzy?
Peter	No. It's just a small cut but it hurts a bit now. Do I have to have stitches?
Doctor	No, it doesn't look that way. I'll just clean and dress it. Are you taking any other medication?
Peter	No.
Doctor	OK, then I can give you some painkillers. They are fairly strong so you mustn't take them with any other types of medicine.
Peter	OK.
Doctor	And come by tomorrow so that I can have a look at the cut and see how you are doing.
Peter	Thanks.

Business communication

Task 8 Work in pairs and tell each other what health and safety regulations there are in your school.

Translation

Task 9

Suggested answers

1. 风险评估就是仔细检查你的工作场所是否有可能对人造成伤害之处，以便你决定是否已采取足够的预防措施或者需要更多措施来防止伤害的发生。
2. 如果检查者询问你的预防措施，或者你有民事责任，则会尤其有效。
3. 无须为每一次微不足道的改变或每一个新工作去修改你的评价。但是如果新工作本身具有很大的新风险，你就要对其进行专门评估并采取一切可能手段来降低风险。
4. 尽管工作提供了经济收益，工作场所的大量风险也对工作人员的健康和安全造成了威胁，这些风险可能是"化学制品、生物制剂、物理因素、恶劣的环境、致敏源、复杂的安全风险网络"和一系列社会心理风险因素。
5. 据观察，2015 年，美国所发生的非致命工作场所伤害事故和疾病呈下降趋势，其中发生在私人企业的有 290 万例，比 2014 年下降了将近 4.8 万例。

Task 10

Suggested answers

1. We will provide a strong guarantee for the operation of the investor's coffee shop through this collaborative project, from the early-stage market assessment, to the mid-term shop design and the late operation support.

2. In our country's construction industry, the phenomenon of the long-time default of the construction contractor's project funds is seriously affecting the healthy and steady development of the industry.
3. As the founder of modern capitalist system, the Dutch had already incorporated banks, credit, insurance, and limited liability companies into an interconnected financial and commercial system by the early 17th century.
4. The brand awareness of the catering enterprises is rather weak, which has resulted in the great difficulty in protecting their rights when encountering similar problems later on. Actually, enterprises can take precautions in advance to prevent the problems from occurring.
5. E-sports have much to do with physical education, education and an array of other departments, which makes it difficult to coordinate a unified official industry standard. The standards issued by major companies are so uneven that they have resulted in today's chaos.

Writing

Task 11

Suggested answer

To: All staff
From: Mr. Port

I would like to inform that due to the recent merger with Mason and Son, our company will be known as MasonGolding. This name becomes official on 17 Sept. 2019. Please note that from this date, the new company name should be used.

Thank you.

Text B

Comprehension tasks

Task 1   T elicits the meaning of court case, plaintiff, judge, and lawsuit. Ss then read the article about a court case and choose the answer.

The meaning of the court case:
The plaintiff lost her case. Although she had mentioned no names on her Facebook page, the company's attorneys were able to convince the judge that the company's reputation had been damaged by the plaintiff complaining about her job online. Sarah, the plaintiff, feels this was an unfair dismissal but is still having problems finding a new job.

Suggested answers
1. d   2. d

Task 2

Suggested answers
1. True
2. False (One of friends told him.)
3. False (Sarah was shocked. She has done the job for the past eight years.)
4. False (Sarah found an attorney and took her company to court.)
5. True
6. True
7. False (Good workers are dismissed and companies will be forced to spend time retraining others to take over these jobs as well as lose their reputations as employee-friendly companies.)

Vocabulary

Task 3

Suggested answers
2. e   3. g   4. a   5. f   6. c   7. d

Task 4

Suggested answers

adjective	noun
justified	justification
absent	absence
possible	possibility
liable	liability
unfair	unfairness

1. unfair   2. absence   3. justified   4. liability   5. possibility

Task 5

Suggested answers

right, unfair dismissal, to be faced with legal action, grievance, to take someone to court, lawyers, attorney, judgement, court case, lawsuit

Unit 6 Work safety and rights

Speaking

Task 6

Suggested answer
The worst three features in my school are first aid facilities, individual work place and washroom facilities. The first aid facilities are seldom used and they have been putting there for over five years. I really wonder if they could work in emergency. Individual work place is something to be improved. No one cleans the offices. The computers won't start. All the furniture is covered with dust. And the washrooms! They are so dirty that it is not easy to go into.

Task 7
T introduces the topic to the Ss by asking them such questions as "Have you or one of you ever be injured at school?", "What is/are the possible reason(s)?", "Who is responsible for the injury?" and "Were you compensated and how?"

Business communication

Task 8
Ss briefly talk about using the Internet and being present on social media sites. (Are you on any social media sites? Are you allowed to use the Internet at work? Do you use social media sites for private or professional purposes?)

Ss discuss the questions about rights and the use of Internet, either T-led or in pairs. T then widens the discussion and leads into the next exercise by asking further questions about laws or regulations in companies regarding Internet use and social media in different places. (What are the regulations for using the Internet at work in your company? How long has this legislation been in operation? How strictly are the rules followed?)

Translation

Task 9

Suggested answers
1. 因为萨拉觉得这些评论不合理，愤怒之下，就在脸书上发表了自己的意见。
2. 他们声称，应该告知所有职员关于使用脸书与那些自己好友栏中好友们聊天而造成的危险后果。
3. 最终这意味着好员工可能会被解雇，公司会被迫花时间培训其他人来接管这些工作，而且公司会失去善待员工的名声。
4. 然而，人们对家装的偏好并没有受到影响，因为喜欢店内购物体验者的比例依旧保持在75%~79%。
5. 劳工支持者和其他团体经常因为工作条件差而批评那些生产车间是血汗工厂，是对职业健康的危害；并在世界各地发起要求改善劳动条件、保障工人权利的运动。

Task 10

> **Suggested answers**
> 1. Under the law, nobody is allowed to force the criminal suspect to disclose details of the case and investigators are not allowed to contact the suspect without the permission from the attorney.
> 2. The regulation of the labour market is rather strict in the European countries with the original intention to protect the labourers' interests, which actually sets up a lot of barriers to the employment and dismissal of employees by enterprises.
> 3. On the one hand, the firemen were still battling against the two big fires; on the other hand, the doctors were striving to save the wounded all night in the hospital temporarily put up.
> 4. Confronted with issues for the company at present, the chairman of board now turns to strategy, cultural affairs and talent cultivating, and focuses more on non-core businesses, after the overall turn-over of the company's operations to the CEO.
> 5. An employee from a real estate agency in Shanghai expressed his favour of the activity, saying that this idea was very original and he needed a festival like this to let off steam when confronted with so much pressure from work.

Writing

Task 11 Ss first formulate an Internet and social media policy which is fair to both management and employees. This may be done in pairs or small groups or as a whole-group activity. T then asks Ss to write a memo informing staff about the policy. Ss write the memo individually, and then exchange memos for feedback about effectiveness and accuracy.

> **Suggested answer**
>
> To: All staff
> From: Charles Dyer
> Date: 7 July 2018
> Re: Internet and social media policy
>
> Management has decided that private use of the Internet during working hours will not be allowed. However, employees who need the Internet for their jobs may continue to use it at work. Furthermore, employees are asked not to publish details of their jobs on social media sites.

Unit 7 Business expenses

Objectives

To enable Ss to talk about expenses
To practise reading for specific information
To practise listening for gist and specific information
To practise memo writing
To practise speaking in groups

Essential vocabulary

Expenses	General
(meal) allowance	to automate
to authorise	component
expense account	due
to claim / claim back (expenses)	limits
claimant	subsequent
to come to (£125)	short notice
to fill in (a form)	urgent
to incur (expenses)	to trial
line manager	worry
to make a (false) claim	
on business	
out of pocket	
to process (a claim)	
receipt	
to reimburse	
small print	

Warming up

Task 1

Suggested answer

I think higher airlines awards for frequent flyers, laptop Powerpoints, and individual entertainment systems are the most important services. Higher airlines awards for frequent flyers should be a matter of course, laptop Powerpoints can help business travellers to work during the trip, and individual entertainment systems can help them to have a good rest.

Unit 7 Business expenses

Task 2

 Suggested answer

I think laptop Powerpoints and in-seat phone facilities can help business people to work. Valet service airport parking, exclusive business lounges, and wider, fully-reclining seats are not necessary for business people. They are only luxuries.

Text A

Comprehension tasks

Task 1

 Suggested answers

1. a   2. b   3. c   4. d   5. e   6. f

Task 2

 Suggested answers

1. True
2. False (They are now also looking into the profitable business travel market segment by expanding their routes and offering a more flexible flight schedule. After adding up various charges, the costs may be the same or even higher than on the mainstream airlines.)
3. True
4. True
5. False (However, a no-frills airline will still have problems competing in areas that business travellers have long taken for granted, in-flight entertainment for example.)
6. False (Because of the problems existing in low-cost airlines concerning in-flight comfort, their policy of undercutting prices, etc., they still have a long way to go to compete with the mainstream airlines regarding business travel.)

Vocabulary

Task 3

 Suggested answers

2. check-in desk
3. scheduled flight
4. in-flight catering
5. reclining seat
6. priority status

Task 4

> **Suggested answers**
> 1. survive 2. complete 3. transfer 4. raise 5. undercut 6. fail

Task 5

> **Suggested answers**
> 1. a 2. c 3. d 4. a 5. a 6. a 7. d 8. c
> 9. b 10. b 11. a 12. c 13. d 14. a 15. d 16. c

Listening

Task 6 T asks Ss to read the three forms to prepare them for the kind of information they need to listen for. Ss then listen to three telephone calls about expenses and fill the gaps in the forms. T needs to remind Ss that only one or two words or a number are needed in each gap; if they wrote more than two words in the exam they would lose points.

> **Suggested answers**
> (1) marketing conference
> (2) £80
> (3) Paul Limbert
> (4) Faxes
> (5) Sweden
> (6) hotel bill
> (7) call him
> (8) earlier payments
> (9) 25-26
> (10) Hotel Continental
> (11) train/Eurostar
> (12) metro tickets

Audioscripts

Conversation 1

David David Hobbs.

Roger Hello, Mr. Hobbs. This is Roger Hargreaves from Accounts. I'm just ringing about your expenses claim. There are a couple of things I need to check.

David OK. What do you need to know?

Roger Well, you put down that it was a business trip. But do you think you could be a bit more specific?

Unit 7 Business expenses

David Yes, sorry. It was actually a marketing conference.
Roger OK. And you stayed at the Cartlands Hotel. But you didn't put down how much it cost.
David Oh, sorry. It was £80. And that was for one night.
Roger I see. Now under "Client Entertaining" you put £56.70 for a meal and drinks. But you are supposed to put down the name of anybody you entertain, you know.
David I'm sorry. I must have forgotten. Anyway, the client's name is Limbert. Paul Limbert. He's one of our Belgian suppliers.
Roger Could you spell his last name for me?
David Limbert? Yes, it's L-I-M-B-E-R-T.
Roger Right, thanks. Oh, and this amount for £9.00 under "Other Expenses". What exactly was that for?
David £9.00? Let me see. £9.00? Oh, yes. That was for a couple of faxes I had to send from the hotel.

Conversation 2

Alison Alison Forbes.
Roger Hello, Alison. It's Roger Hargreaves from Accounts. Is Alan there, please?
Alison I'm afraid he isn't in today. Can I help at all?
Roger I don't think so, no. It's about his expenses, you know, for the trip to Sweden.
Alison Can I give him a message?
Roger Yes, if you could. Could you tell him that something was missing? It was his hotel bill. And I need it quickly if he wants us to pay him this month.
Alison Actually, I think he was looking for it the other day.
Roger I hope he hasn't lost it. Well, look, if he can't find it, he really needs to call me as soon as possible.
Alison OK. I'll tell him.
Roger Thanks. Oh, and one other thing. The last time we paid him his expenses, he asked us to pay him before our pay date. Well, I'm afraid it caused all kinds of problems, and everyone started asking for earlier payments. So we've decided that we really can't do that again.
Alison OK, I'll let him know. Bye.

Conversation 3

Chris Hello?
Roger Hello, Mr. Evans?
Chris Speaking.
Roger This is Roger Hargreaves. I'm just ringing about your expenses for the Paris trip.
Chris Well, did you know the airline lost my suitcase on that trip? And unfortunately, some of my receipts were in it.
Roger But you still have some of them? I just need to check a few details.
Chris OK. What do you need to know?
Roger Well, first of all, when was the trip exactly?

Chris	Let me just check my diary. Yes, it was the last weekend in June. The 25th and 26th.
Roger	So one night. Right. And where did you stay?
Chris	Hotel Continental. My original booking information was in my suitcase but I've got my credit card receipt. However, it's in Euros. Is it better to wait till my credit card bill comes? Then you'll have it in pounds sterling.
Roger	That's fine. I'll see that when it comes in. You put it on the company card, didn't you?
Chris	Yes.
Roger	What about travel? Did you fly or take the train?
Chris	The train. Eurostar. I have my ticket but I don't have all the other booking information.
Roger	That's fine. I can check that myself. Oh, and were there any other expenses?
Chris	I can't think of anything. Oh, yes there was actually. I had to buy metro tickets to get around Paris and the receipts for those were in my luggage.
Roger	Metro tickets... that'd be about six euros a day wouldn't it?
Chris	That sounds about right.
Roger	OK, Mr. Evans, thanks very much.

Task 7

Suggested answers

1. f   2. a   3. d   4. g   5. e

Audioscripts

Call 1	Good morning. This is a message for David Eastman. I got your note about my expenses form—about returning it to you. Well, actually I did send it to you. The only problem is it went to the wrong department, and that's why you still haven't got it. Anyway, I'll bring it round first thing in the morning, OK? Oh, sorry, this is Alex Eddington, by the way.
Call 2	Hello, this is June Salisbury. You wanted to speak to me about my expenses claim for the Munich trip. Could we get together on Friday morning to talk about it? Perhaps at about 11, if that's all right? Just give my secretary a call. OK. Bye.
Call 3	This is Bob Richards here. Listen, I've just found another receipt for my Oslo trip last month. It's for quite a lot of photocopies I had done in a shop. I suppose it's too late for this month, but is it OK if I put this through on next month's expenses? Could you get back to me and let me know? OK. Bye.
Call 4	Hello, this is Patricia Graves from Sales. I'm ringing about my expenses again. The last time I called you, you said they'd be included in this month's pay. Well, I've checked my payslip and they haven't been paid yet. I have another trip coming up and am not happy about being out of pocket. Can you please get back to me and let me know when I can expect to be reimbursed for my outlays on the last trip? Thanks.

Call 5 Hello, David. This is Simon. Look, about this morning to discuss limits on client entertainment, I'm afraid something urgent's come up and I have to rush off to London, so I won't be able to make it. I'm really sorry it's such short notice. I'll call you when I get back. OK? Speak to you soon.

Business communication

Task 8 T asks Ss to read the three situations. Ss discuss what they would do, working in pairs or as a group. T elicits the reasons for Ss' responses.

Translation

Task 9

Suggested answers
1. 有几家航空公司正在准备通过扩大航线、提供更加灵活的航行时间表来挤身利润丰厚的商务旅行市场。
2. 商务旅行者是否愿意用包装三明治和普通饮用水来替换优质的食品服务和多种饮料的选择当然是值得怀疑的。
3. 如果商务旅行者不得不付费上厕所、排队才能坐上自己想坐的座位，或者自己拎着午餐上飞机，那么他们中的绝大部分会宁愿乘坐主流航空公司的班机。
4. 除了12个头等座和301个在（客机）下层的经济座，大韩航空公司还指定客机的整个上层（94座）为商务舱。
5. 在穿过巴塞罗那机场回家的路上，我只需展示手机上的虚拟登机牌就通过了登机口而无须出示任何纸质文件——除了一本护照。

Task 10

Suggested answers
1. Although the world's situation is constantly changing and uncertainty becomes the norm, peaceful development is still the mainstream of the world, and cooperation and mutual benefits have become a global consensus.
2. Though the railway company has exerted the greatest efforts in the past few months, it still fails to provide a satisfactory explanation to the public for the rise of business class fares.
3. The theme of this marketing symposium is to learn from and to carry forward the advanced experience from those with sound morality and excellent performance, to summarize, reflect on and address the problems, and make concerted effort in order to improve operation efficiency.
4. The Wuling vans and minivans are very popular among the light commercial vehicle buyers and the farmer buyers, and their price is only a small fraction of that of the American vehicles.

5. Excellent enterprises should focus on the making of quality products at low prices, and make every cent paid by users value-for-money.

Writing

Task 11

Suggested answer

Dear Mr Chandler,

Re: Order No. B13/4620

Thank you for your letter dated 28 June. First of all, I would like to apologise for the unsatisfactory handling of your order.

Unfortunately, all our deliveries have experienced delays because of a strike by lorry drivers. However, as this dispute has now been settled, I am pleased to inform you that we will be able to replace the two damaged desks next week.

As for the invoice, as an established and valued customer you should have automatically received a discount of 10%. I enclose an amended invoice and trust that you will accept a further 2% discount for the inconvenience you have experienced.

I would like to take this opportunity to assure you that any future orders will be dealt with reliably and efficiently.

Yours sincerely,

Text B

Comprehension tasks

Task 1

Suggested answers

1. A corporate charge card (Amex), and an automated online expenses reimbursement system with automatic updates to a personal expense account.
2. It will eliminate the need for cash advances, reduce administrative time, reduce the cost of processing claims and reduce the time employees spend on claiming expenses.
3. Charges to the company credit card for business travel will be automatically updated to a personal account.
4. Employees need to log in to their accounts and fill in the relevant details, including codes about airlines and hotels.

Unit 7 Business expenses

5. They need to supply information about guests including names and companies.
6. They will receive automatic requests for information.
7. The system has built-in limits for client entertainment and meal allowances.
8. They are to hold to use a private credit card.

Task 2

Suggested answers
1. c   2. b

Vocabulary

Task 3

Suggested answers
2. scan receipts
3. reimburse expenses
4. implementing, system
5. processing claims
6. log in to, account

Task 4

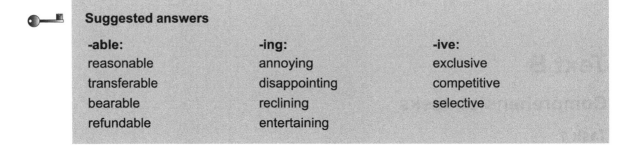

Suggested answers

-able:	-ing:	-ive:
reasonable	annoying	exclusive
transferable	disappointing	competitive
bearable	reclining	selective
refundable	entertaining	

Task 5

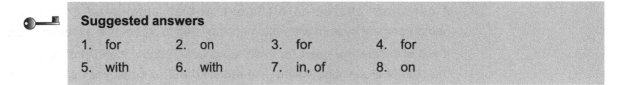

Suggested answers
1. for   2. on   3. for   4. for
5. with   6. with 7. in, of 8. on

Speaking

Task 6 T asks Ss to work in pairs and tell each other in turn about some of their experiences of air travel. They may start by talking about the services, the fare, the comfort, the food, etc., which are provided by the airlines.

If they have never travelled by air, they can tell their travelling experiences by other means.

Task 7 T asks Ss to talk about this question by comparing the advantages and disadvantages of both the mainstream and low-cost airlines, such as the flight schedule, cost, direct or indirect flights, in-flight entertainment and comfort, foods provided, etc.

Business communication

Task 8 Ss describe the system for claiming expenses in their company or another institution, if they know it, and suggest improvements. They may start from such aspects as whether the system works efficiently or not, whether the procedures are complicated or not, whether the time duration is long or short, etc.

Translation

Task 9

Suggested answers

1. 对于处理公司商务旅行支出及其报销的替换系统，我们部门已经做了大量的调查。
2. 它还将降低处理每一单报销的成本，员工在报销时也会节约大量时间。
3. 因为系统中有内置的对于客户娱乐和宴请补贴的数额限制，所以发生这些费用的话，你最好及时报销掉。
4. 信用卡可以向卖方保证该卡的使用者拥有良好的信用等级，并且该信用卡的发卡行也能担保卖方能收到所卖商品的款项。
5. 随着利润的大幅度下降，大多数企业都在试图削减管理成本，有些企业甚至在考虑合并事宜。

Task 10

Suggested answers

1. This pet insurance project requires clients to pay in advance the bills for pet's medical care, and then make the reimbursement after submitting receipts.
2. After six months of constant consultation, the two parties finally signed a framework agreement of economic cooperation, which would be implemented step by step in the following ten years.
3. The original design structure was thoroughly changed, and the architectural designers made full use of independent space and built-in furniture in planning and segmenting the apartment.
4. This laptop offers all-day-long battery life, whether it is for daily office work, or long time entertainment, or online video watching, or web surfing and social network chatting.
5. When joining group tour, you must ask for the agreement, the itinerary and the receipt of items. Otherwise, it will be very difficult for you to make complaints for lack of evidence and your personal safety cannot be guaranteed.

Writing

Task 11

Suggested answer

Thursday 24 May

10:40 Arrive Frankfurt airport. We will arrange for a taxi to meet you and bring you straight to the company.

11:30 Tour of the company.

12:30 Lunch with Mirijana Krutz.

14:00 Visit SKA GmbH in Wiesbaden. (Return to hotel by 17:00.)

20:00 Dinner with Pierre Bonner.

Friday 25 May

09:00 Visit Kahn & Sohn, a supplier.

13:00 Lunch in Frankfurt.

14:30 Meeting with MD Michael Thomas and Sales Director Suzanna Kopke. (to finish at about 17:00.)

We have booked your return flight for Saturday morning at 08:40. You will need to confirm this flight 24 hours in advance. If you have any questions, please do not hesitate to contact us.

We look forward to seeing you soon.

Unit 8 Staff appraisal

> **Objectives**
>
> To enable Ss to talk about appraisals
> To practise reading for specific information
> To practise listening for gist

Essential vocabulary

Appraisals	General
to appraise (employees)	to air grievances
appeal process	to cause (concern)
to assume responsibility	corporate strategy
delegation skills	current
to evaluate (performance)	to define (duties/roles)
(to give/get) feedback	exchange ideas
job description	to fail (to respond)
to meet (aims/objectives/deadlines)	to hire
to miss (targets/deadlines)	to ignore
(training) policy	instance
promotion	internal vacancy
prospects	qualification
	to set joint projects
	to subsidise

Warming up

Task 1

> **Suggested answer**
>
> Staff appraisal is an important part of human resource management, and its purpose is to monitor staff's performance.

Task 2

Suggested answer

The three most important reasons for staff appraisals are to review and evaluate past performance, to help improve current performance, and to set future performance objectives. To review and evaluate the past performance will help to identify what needs to be improved, such as clarifying staff's duties and responsibilities. To improve the current performance will make the company remain invincible, and these will help to set more reasonable objectives.

Text A

Comprehension tasks

Task 1

Suggested answers

1. c   2. b   3. c   4. a   5. c   6. d

Task 2

Suggested answers

1. True
2. False — They view the process as a necessary evil.
3. False — It is possible, and in some cases more suitable, to arrange appraisals where performance is rated for the group.
4. True
5. True
6. True

Vocabulary

Task 3

Suggested answers

1. exchange   2. air   3. meet   4. evaluated
5. responsibilities   6. promotion   7. update   8. policy

Task 4

Suggested answers

Verb	Noun
appraise	appraisal
criticise	criticism
notify	notification
assign	assignment
approve	approval
develop	development
permit	permission
evaluate	evaluation

2. notification
3. evaluate
4. development
5. criticism
6. permit
7. approve
8. assign

Task 5

Suggested answers

2. d   3. e   4. c   5. a

Listening

Task 6

Suggested answers

(1) managed   (2) get round   (3) busy
(4) form   (5) difficulties   (6) admit
(7) how it goes   (8) the first thing   (9) research project
(10) deadline   (11) regional offices   (12) asking for information
(13) the rest of the team   (14) colleagues   (15) visiting
(16) comes to an end

Audioscripts

Maureen	So, Dexter, we've finally managed to find time for your appraisal. I'm sorry I've been so slow to get round to it.
Dexter	That's OK. Everyone seems to be so busy right now.
Maureen	Yes, they do. It's that time of year again. isn't it? Anyway, we're here now. Did you remember to bring your appraisal form?
Dexter	Here it is.
Maureen	Did you have any difficulties in filling it in?
Dexter	Not really, though I must admit not being too sure about one or two bits of it.
Maureen	That's OK. Should we just start working our way through it from the beginning and see how it goes?
Dexter	Yeah. Sure.
Maureen	So, the first thing is what you've been doing over the last 12 months. So what do we have here...
Dexter	Well, as you can see, it's mainly been the Service2012 research project.
Maureen	On, yes. And how's it going?
Dexter	Fine. I don't want to sound too confident, but we should manage to meet next month's deadline without too much difficulty.
Maureen	Well, that's good. Well done. And was it difficult to get all the information together that you needed?
Dexter	We've been very lucky not to have had any problems. All the regional offces have been really helpful and cooperative. It would've been a lot harder to get all the data we needed if they hadn't been so helpful. There were one or two offices that we had to keep asking for information, but on the whole everyone was very cooperative.
Maureen	That's great. And what was it like working with the rest of the team?
Dexter	Fine. They're all really easy to get on with. I've enjoyed working with them. Meeting colleagues from other offices has been very interesting. You find out all sorts of things about the company.
Maureen	I bet you do.
Dexter	I quite enjoyed travelling around the country a bit and visiting the other offices too. I think I'll quite miss working on the Service 2012 team when the project comes to an end next month.
Maureen	In terms of development, what do you think you've learnt fom...

Task 7

Suggested answer

Q: What have you been doing over the last twelve months?

A: We have been doing the Service 2012 research project.

Q: How's it going?

A: It's going fine, but we should manage to meet the deadline next month.

> Q: Was it difficult to get all the information together that you needed?
>
> A: We've been very lucky not having had any problems. All the regional offices have been really helpful and co-operative.
>
> Q: What was it like working with the rest of the team?
>
> A: Fine. They're all really easy to get on with. I've enjoyed working with them.

Business communication

Task 8   Ss are encouraged to give specific examples.

> **Suggested answer**
>
> The outcome of this exercise will differ depending on whether Ss are in-work or pre-work.
>
> **In-work Ss would:**
> - Know where they are going and what they want in the future.
> - Think carefully about what duties, responsibilities they should take up to achieve the goals.
> - Consider the most difficult and most interesting parts on the way to the goals.
>
> **Pre-work Ss should:**
> - Think about the type of job they hope to have as their career in the future.
> - Consider the duties and responsibilities.
> - Try to imagine what will be the most difficult or most interesting parts in their future career.

Translation

Task 9

> **Suggested answers**
> 1. 无论你询问任何公司中任何级别的任何雇员对工作的不满意之处，你都会听到对绩效考核制度的抱怨。
> 2. 对绩效考核制度的抱怨主要有两大类：其一是对考核制度本身的不满，其二是关于考核制度的实施和理解。
> 3. 比如，如果员工常常以团队合作的形式工作，共同为成败承担责任，那么对个人的绩效考评就没有意义了，这只会导致怨恨和团队的分裂。
> 4. 绩效考核通常将员工的工作成绩与其岗位标准或目标进行比较，它主要分为非正式考核和正式的绩效考核两种形式。
> 5. 在集团人力资源总监和员工研究与考评部门领导的指导下，苏格兰皇家银行的人力资源部门通过打造其"人力资本模式"正在全公司创造一种凝心聚力的公司环境和文化。

Task 10

Suggested answers

1. Commodity prices have been going down from last quarter. He still believes that this trend cannot be reversed, even though there is a slight upward tendency.
2. This case highlights the existing dispute between major companies and the government. The company takes it as its primary responsibility to protect its users' privacy, while the supervising department maintains that public security comes before the privacy of the users.
3. Enterprises have to change the practice of relationship and seniority orientation, to carry out the practice of capability assessment and performance appraisal, and to set up a long-term incentive and restrain mechanism.
4. With underlying problems unsolved, this decision which will determine the development of the company in the future five years cannot be implemented successfully.
5. We earnestly promise that we will continue to maintain and promote regional peace, security and stability, seek peaceful settlement of disputes, respect and choose legal and diplomatic means, and will not resort to threat or use of force.

Writing

Task 11

Suggested answer

(To all managers)
(Subject: Staff Appraisals)

I would like to remind you that you should be holding your staff appraisals this month. Once you have completed them, could you please send me a copy of each report? If you would like to use an interview room, please remember to reserve it in advance.

Thank you.

Text B

Comprehension tasks

Task 1

Suggested answers

1. b   2. d   3. a   4. b   5. c

Task 2

Suggested answers

1. False — The first speaker is talking about workload.
2. True
3. True
4. False — The fourth speaker received more criticism than compliments from her boss.
5. False — The fifth speaker isn't sure whether they'd be able to repeat last year's performance.

Vocabulary

Task 3

Suggested answers

2. She's co-ordinating the project and setting the group's objectives.
3. We're working towards unrealistic targets.
4. She'll really have to concentrate on meeting her objectives.
5. Did he achieve his target last month?
6. Could we please review my sales target for the current year?
7. We've set ourselves a range of objectives for the coming year.

Task 4

Suggested answers

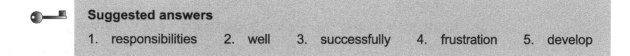

1. responsibilities   2. well   3. successfully   4. frustration   5. develop

Task 5

Suggested answers

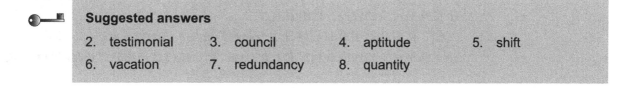

2. testimonial   3. council   4. aptitude   5. shift
6. vacation   7. redundancy   8. quantity

Speaking

Task 6   Ss work in pair and discuss one or more of the 6 questions from the form.

Unit 8   Staff appraisal

Task 7

Suggested answer

Speaker 1   is concerned with his workload and hopes to hand over some of his work to colleagues in order to concentrate on the things he was hired to do.

Speaker 2   is concerned with her study for a management qualification and her boss would support her and subsidise the cost because her training will benefit both herself and the company.

Speaker 3   hopes to apply for an internal vacancy because she has been doing the same job for five years.

Speaker 4   is complaining about his boss. His boss is misunderstanding him and he is not getting enough support from the management.

Speaker 5   is more concerned with the ridiculous objectives her boss has set for them. Management was carried away by last year's success and they expect more from the speaker and her team.

Business communication

Task 8   Ss rank themselves according to given criteria.

Translation

Task 9

Suggested answers

1. 在我们一起讨论了该如何更清晰地划分我们的职责之后，她同意我把部分工作转交给其他同事。
2. 我也提到了我曾申请过几个公司内部的招聘岗位，但都以失败告终。
3. 在经历过一个成功的年度之后，唯一的问题就是管理层往往会忘乎所以，总希望一直会有奇迹发生。
4. 企业责任意识不仅会带来更大的职业满足感、更强烈的幸福感，而且能在一定程度上提高对员工的管控，杜绝蒙混过关。
5. 尽管一些管理写手有时会将日本企业的劳资关系描绘得异常美好，索尼公司的管理理念是把员工当作同事和帮助者来对待，而不仅仅是当作公司获取利润的手段。

Task 10

Suggested answers

1. With the gradual economic recovery, the rate of land vacancy is declining, and the land price and rental price have a significant rebound in the whole country.
2. Rather than committing itself to the overall improvement of public welfare, the government is vigorously subsidising individuals and businesses with low-paying jobs at present.

3. This Internet company specially recruited a group of people, whose job is to delete those posts and videos that are considered "negative to the company" with the deadline of an hour after they are posted.
4. We appeal to all countries for mutual respect, equal consultations, and closer cooperation. We are opposed to trade war and price war, because they are not in the interest of any party.
5. As a model of successful entrepreneurship of the generation born in the 1980s, she said that although she had made some progresses, it was still necessary for her to keep a clear mind because she didn't want to get carried away by her achievements.

Writing

Task 11

Suggested answer

To: Lisa Bradley
From: Mary Parker
Re: Invoice No. 21692

Dear Mr. Bradley,

I apologise for the delay in paying the above invoice. This is due to a computer error in our Accounts Department. I can assure you that the invoice will be paid in full today.

Case study Cash flow

> **Objectives**
>
> To enable Ss to talk about day-to-day company finances
> To practise reading for specific information
> To practise listening for specific information
> To practise note writing

Essential vocabulary

Finance	General
cash flow	bar chart
inflow	to benefit
outflow	case study
cash on delivery	components
credit terms	to install
down payment	installation
early settlement discount	inventory
to finance	shortage
financing costs	
interest	
labour costs	
(profit) margin	
net	
order book	
outstanding balance	
over-trading	
(late) payment	
penalty charges	
sales price	
turnover	
wages	

Warming up

Task 1   Ss briefly discuss what inflows and outflows companies have. (Inflows refer to all the money coming into the company, like income from sales, whereas outflows refer to all the money going out of the company, like wages.) The concept of inflow and outflow needs to be clear so that Ss understand the concept of cash flow and the case study.

Task 2

Suggested answer

Inexperience of the entrepreneurs; instability of human resource; shortage of funds; technique limitation on production; disputes among investors and in-fighting.

Case: The cash flow gap

Comprehension tasks

Task 1

Suggested answers

1. d   2. c

Task 2

Ss scan the text for the words listed and say whether they refer to inflows or outflows in the Quick Computers case study.

Suggested answer

Inflows: down payment, total sales price, outstanding balance

Outflows: early settlement discount*, labour costs, wages, to finance, interest

(*Early settlement discount is a reduction off an outflow. Ss might therefore argue it is an inflow.)

Vocabulary

Task 3

Suggested answer

People
payee, creditor, adviser, cashier, banker

Papers
advice note, paying-in slip, counterfoil, statement

Account management
credit, deduct, transaction, interest, deposit, debit

Task 4

Suggested answers

2. g   3. i   4. f   5. h
6. a   7. j   8. c   9. e   10. d

Task 5

Suggested answers

1. CORRECT
2. THROUGH
3. US
4. IT
5. THE
6. CORRECT
7. BEEN
8. MOST
9. WHICH
10. CORRECT
11. ARE
12. BE
13. CORRECT
14. A
15. CORRECT

Listening and speaking

Task 6

Suggested answers

(1) why I'm here
(2) papers
(3) growing
(4) nature
(5) fulfill
(6) finance
(7) figures
(8) what to say

Audioscripts

Faiza	Michael. Nice to see you again. Come in. How's business?
Michael	Hi Faiza. Business isn't too good, I'm afraid. That's why I'm here.
Faiza	OK. Well, sit down and let's see what we are going to do about it.
Michael	Thanks. I'll just get some papers out and then I can show you what the problem is.
Faiza	OK. I'll get my glasses. How many people do you have working for you now?
Michael	Thirty-six but two people are starting on Monday.
Faiza	Wow. That's great. Things are growing really quickly.
Michael	It gets busy at this time of year. It always does about now. It's the nature of the business.
Faiza	Are you taking on any more people over the summer?
Michael	I'd like to but I don't think we'll be able to afford it. But without the extra workers, we won't fulfill all the orders we already have, not to mention any new ones.
Faiza	Oh, I see.
Michael	I'll definitely need to raise some finance somehow over the summer so I can take on more workers. And that's why I'm here. Do you think the bank will lend me some more money?
Faiza	Whatever they do, they'll want to take a close look at these figures to see how your business is doing.
Michael	I know. I'm seeing my bank manager next week. I've got an appointment on Thursday. So I thought maybe you could look at these figures for me and advise me on what to say at the bank.
Faiza	Sure. I'll see what I can do.
Michael	Thanks, Faiza, It won't be easy on Monday and I think I'll need all the help I can get.

Task 7

T asks Ss briefly what inflows and outflows companies have. (Inflows refer to all the money coming into the company, like income from sales, whereas outflows refer to all the money going out of the company, like wages.) The concept of inflow and outflow needs to be clear so that Ss understand the concept of cash flow and the case study.

Business communication

Task 8

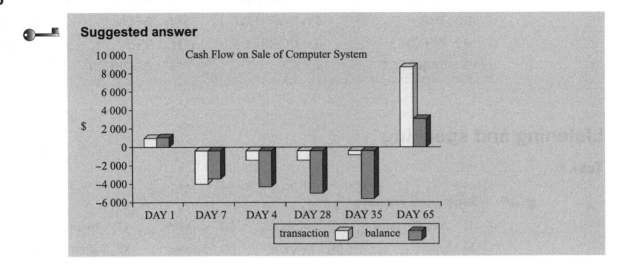

Suggested answer

Translation

Task 9

Suggested answers

1. 当客户下单之后，史蒂夫要收总价的 10% 作为预付定金。
2. 如果史蒂夫收货之后 10 天之内付款，这个供应商愿意提供 2% 的折扣。
3. 这意味着在客户付清 9 000 美元之前，他还要筹措 5 920 美元并且为此付 30 天的利息。
4. 主要是由于劳动成本的缘故，我们认为将智能手机或服装的供应链搬到美国至少要花 5 年时间。
5. 从 1990 年到 2015 年，美国公司在中国投资将近 2 300 亿美元；同期中国企业在美国投资 640 亿美元。这说明中美之间的经济联系这些年来一直在增长。

Task 10

Suggested answers

1. Roughly calculated, the number of the Vietnamese who cross the border to work in Yi-cheng Foodstuff Co. Ltd., Dong-xing, Guangxi Province, is over 300, and the wage here is very attractive to the Vietnamese.
2. The different units of the university are distributed in the urban area, without walls as a whole. However, each school has its own fences and most of them are not free to open to visitors.
3. Since this is the first deal, we offer you a special 1% discount.
4. This contract will go into effect automatically after the seller has received 30% of the total sales price as down payment from the buyer, which is stipulated in Article 5.1 of the contract.

5. In the five years to come, Xiong'an New Area will ensure the investment transparency and the active environmental benefit by means of green finance, and carry out urban infrastructure construction by taking advantage of billions of investment.

Writing

Task 11

Suggested answer

Dear all,

As Mr Tilde is going to retire next month, we have hired Ms. Bianchi from Nesco, PLC to take the position of Sales Manager. She will join us on 1 April. Please help her with any questions she may have.

Carol Smith

Analysis: Improving cash flow

Comprehension tasks

Task 1

Suggested answers

1. d   2. c

Task 2

Suggested answers

1. Over-trading.
2. About half.
3. Their margins are already small; they can't afford to offer discounts.
4. $25,000.
5. Financing costs.
6. $500.
7. They would have an extra $16,000 a month.
8. They decide to offer a 1% early settlement discount.

Vocabulary

Task 3

Suggested answers

- We can offer you a cash discount of 2%.
- Some customers pay cash on delivery.
- The cash price is 1% lower than the normal price.
- We can pay in cash or give you a cheque.
- Their cash flow situation is getting worse.
- We can't pay until the end of the month because of a cash shortage.
- He made a cash payment of $2,000 when he placed his order.
- If his cash forecast is correct, we'll need to see the bank about a loan.

Task 4

Suggested answers

1. a tax payer – income tax – the government
2. a bank – interest on savings – an account holder
3. an importer – customs duty – the government
4. the government – tax relief – a tax payer
5. an account holder – bank charges – a bank
6. a company – a dividend – shareholders

Task 5

Suggested answers

1. year   2. payment   3. transaction   4. discount   5. cash
6. note   7. code   8. condition   9. cheque   10. duty

Speaking

Task 6

Suggested answer

The major problem with Quick Computers is over-trading: the more they sell, the less cash they seem to have. The problem means that before a low-budget company receives all revenue from selling its service (or a product) it will not be able to absorb all cost for providing the service (or production), making its cash flow situation difficult. As over-trading goes, it becomes more difficult to cover the cost. Usually under such conditions, companies have to either seek for financing or pressing for a quick payment from their clients.

Task 7 Ss discuss the advantages and disadvantages of discount and give their opinions on discount.

Business communication

Task 8 In pairs Ss choose the best ideas and discuss how they would benefit the company (e.g. If Quick Computers increased prices, sales might decrease. This might help the cash flow problem but doesn't seem a good idea in general.). In feedback T elicits suggestions and checks Ss are using conditional forms accurately.

Translation

Task 9

Suggested answers
1. 你得找到一个更快的方法将这些销售变现。
2. 填补现金流缺口意味着你一年付给银行的利息将达到近 3 000 美金。
3. 史蒂夫，如果我是你的话，我肯定会认真考虑提供一个提前付款折扣。
4. 美国在运输和农产品等市场上对中国保持贸易顺差。
5. 全球汽车市场的销售额从 2005 年的 6 400 万辆增加到了 2015 年的 8 800 万辆，增长了 3%；而同期内，中国市场的销售额从 500 万辆增加到了 2 400 万辆，市场份额从 8% 增长到了 28%。

Task 10

Suggested answers
1. False advertisements always exaggerate, which will not only cause losses for consumers but also jeopardize the company's reputation and margin, and affect the public trust.
2. The bank's information shows that the company may be caught by risks of over-trading because it needs a large number of working capital at every round of development and expansion.
3. A leader should figure out ways to turn his own sense of crisis into the organisation members'. Once this is realised, the organization will remain invincible.
4. He hoped that his vote would make a difference for people, at least on securing fundamental education and health care.
5. In China where the per capita water availability on average is lower than one fourth of that of the world's average, the water pollution in some areas intensifies scarcity of water resources, which has made a negative impact on the ecological system, food supply and public sanitation.

Writing

Task 11 Ss compose a reply of 40–50 words which contains the three points listed. In pairs Ss present their draft to each other and offer feedback on the clarity, length and formality of the reply. T should make the point, reinforced in the writing tip, that although emails are often short and informal, no particular style is required; the style depends on the writer's relationship with the reader.

Suggested answer

Hi Steve,

It's good to know that business is going well. Of course I'll help! I think Sue's idea could be one solution but wait and let's discuss it together in more detail. How about a meeting on Friday at 10 a.m. in my office? See you then.

Barbara

Review Test 2

Part I Listening comprehension

Task 1

> **Suggested answers**
> 1. Unit 5
> 2. Office Manager
> 3. photocopy paper
> 4. Thursday

Audioscripts

Initial Business Supplies	Initial Business Supplies. Good morning.
Lacey Graphics	Good morning. This is Lacey Graphics. I'd like to place an order, please.
Initial Business Supplies	OK. I'll just get an order form. Right. Now, it's Lacey Graphics?
Lacey Graphics	That's right. We have an account with you.
Initial Business Supplies	Sorry. I didn't know. I'm new here.
Lacey Graphics	Oh, that's OK.
Initial Business Supplies	Could you give me your address, please?
Lacey Graphics	Yes, of course. It's 23 Long Edge Road, Hailsham.
Initial Business Supplies	And that's the delivery address?
Lacey Graphics	Could you mark it Unit 5, please?
Initial Business Supplies	And could I have your name, please?
Lacey Graphics	Well, I'm Liz Price, but I'd like you to address it to the "Office Manager", please.
Initial Business Supplies	OK. Fine. Now what's the order for?
Lacey Graphics	We'd like ten boxes of high-quality A4 paper for the photocopier as well as another fifteen boxes of pencils and eight of pens.
Initial Business Supplies	I'm afraid we're out of the pencils and pens at the moment but I can send you the photocopy paper and call you when the pens and pencils come in and we can deal with the order then. Is that OK?
Lacey Graphics	Yes, that'll be fine.
Initial Business Supplies	And when would you like it?
Lacey Graphics	Well, as soon as possible, really. We've nearly run out.
Initial Business Supplies	Let's see, I could get it to you by Friday, no actually Thursday should work if you prefer.
Lacey Graphics	That's great. Thanks.
Initial Business Supplies	And how will you be paying?
Lacey Graphics	Well, you usually send us an invoice.
Initial Business Supplies	OK. And that's to the same address?
Lacey Graphics	That's right.

Task 2

Suggested answers

1. f   2. e   3. g   4. a   5. h

Audioscripts

1. So, two of the boxes were damaged. And they were the ones with the A3 paper in them. I'm afraid we don't have any more of that in stock. But we've got a delivery coming tomorrow. So we'll send you two new boxes as soon as we can, if that's OK.
2. Well, if you can wait a while, there's something coming up in the next few weeks. Now I haven't seen it myself, but I've been told by the owners that it should be ready for immediate occupation. So, as long as you can work out the finance and insurance in time, you should be in by the start of next month. And it's a lot cheaper than the other site you were considering.
3. Yes, we can arrange it now, if you'd like, if you want to pay by credit card. And if time's the most important factor, then that's what I'd recommend. That way, we can guarantee it'll arrive by 8:30 tomorrow morning. But somebody will have to sign for it, of course.
4. The way it works is that we negotiate an agreed limit with you, say £400. Now if you use this facility, there's a flat monthly charge of £5, and then there's the interest on the overdraft as well, of course, which is 17.5% at the moment. If you do find that this amount doesn't meet your needs, you can always come in and we can look at the situation again.
5. You can organise your insurance through us—against accidents, theft and loss of baggage for the duration of the trip. We use Non-Stop, a leading company in the business. We find their rates very competitive. So, for two weeks that'll be £34. Shall I just add the premium on to the fare?

Task 3

Suggested answers

1. c   2. b   3. c   4. a
5. b   6. c   7. a   8. c

Audioscripts

Bill, Interviewer	Good morning everyone. I'm here with Jilliana Patal who is going to talk to us about how supermarkets are looking into enhancing their green images.
Jilliana Patal	Good morning, Bill. Well, this has been very interesting to watch. As I am sure you know, supermarkets have never been known for being green proponents. After all, they sell large numbers of packaged goods imported from around the world and look for the lowest prices they can offer.
Bill, Interviewer	That's true. That's an argument that the organisers of farmers' markets have had for years.
Jilliana Patal	Yes, that is why following this has been so interesting. Just this month one of the major chains in the U.K. has promised to reduce their waste and promote fair-trade products in the shops. In addition, they plan to make the company what they are calling "carbon neutral".

Bill, Interviewer	What do they mean by that?
Jilliana Patal	They plan to balance the amount of carbon they produce with the amount they use. In other words, they want to find ways to use up carbon such as planting trees or growing produce.
Bill, Interviewer	That's really interesting. And just think, if the other major chains followed suit, this could mean huge steps in the direction of creating a sustainable society.
Jilliana Patal	Exactly. And as you pointed out, this particular company is the only one to do this. Another major supermarket chain has already come out with a plan to cut their carbon dioxide emissions from its operations. In addition, they will be adding carbon labels to all products so that consumers can immediately see how much carbon was created to produce and transport the product. This helps to make the public responsible consumers as well and they can then make an educated decision about which product they want to buy.
Bill, Interviewer	Really innovative I would say. It seems that this is the next logical extension of nutritional labelling.
Jilliana Patal	Yes, it is. Other plans include making green alternatives more affordable. Starting by selling an everyday household item such as low-energy light bulbs at half price.
Bill, Interviewer	Why is all this taking place?
Jilliana Patal	Well, I think that there are different motivations behind all of this. Some chains have always strived to be high-end, high-price retailers. They realise that joining in the green revolution will help their brand and encourage customer loyalty. After all, a large part of the affluent market is concerned about climate change and sustainability issues. And as many of them are also the decision-makers in politics or business, marketing the idea to them is simply a good strategy to keep them as customers as well as spokespeople for the brand.
Bill, Interviewer	And the other shops?
Jilliana Patal	Well, the lower priced shops may have a different agenda. They may be getting some pressure from their customers, but they are more worried about media coverage and even possibly having problems with expansion plans or operating licenses. They need to look carefully at their CSR, or corporate social responsibility image if they want to continue to grow.
Bill, Interviewer	It seems today that tackling the problem of climate change is becoming a major part of leadership in business.
Jilliana Patal	Exactly. And don't forget that competition is still the name of the game. If one major company puts itself out there as the leader in creating a sustainable future, the others won't be able to afford to continue as they have been. The PR resulting from these changes can take over and create negative publicity for those ignoring the call to help the planet. And don't forget how quickly word spreads today through the Internet and the incredibly powerful use of social media.
Bill, Interviewer	That's true. It seems that peer pressure may help where regulations were not able to. Thanks for talking to us today, Jilliana. It will be interesting to see what happens in this area in the future.

Part II Reading and writing

Task 4

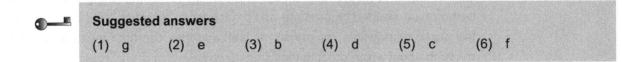

Suggested answers

1. c	2. d	3. a	4. a	5. a
6. d	7. c	8. b	9. b	10. a
11. c	12. d	13. a	14. d	15. c

Task 5

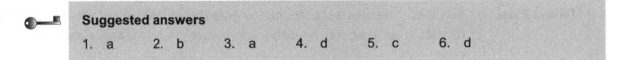

Suggested answers

(1) g   (2) e   (3) b   (4) d   (5) c   (6) f

Task 6

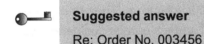

Suggested answers

1. a   2. b   3. a   4. d   5. c   6. d

Task 7

Suggested answer

Re: Order No. 003456

Dear Ms. Wilson,

Thank you for the order which we received today. Unfortunately, there are problems with the order that I would like to bring to your attention.

Firstly, the quantity of small ladies' jeans (cat No. JNW606M) is incorrect. We ordered 400 units but received only 200 units. Could you please send the remaining part of the order as soon as possible?

Secondly, about 20 packets of the men's T-shirts (cat No. TSM40XL) arrived damaged. The delivery company says bad packaging allowed them to get wet. We therefore ask you to replace these items.

We have had problems with several deliveries from you recently. I am sure you understand that it is essential for our business that orders arrive on time, correctly and in good condition. If you can not guarantee this, then I am afraid we will have to consider alternative suppliers.

I look forward to hearing from you soon.

Part III Business knowledge and translation

Task 8

Suggested answers

1. intellectual property

    Definition: Something such as an invention or a copyright which is officially owned by someone, such as patent, copyright and trademark. Same as properties owned by people and protected by laws, intellectual property contains in itself a value that could be traded for a profit.

    Translation: 知识产权

2. unilateral liberalisation

    Definition: Also referred as unilateral trade liberalisation, it means the process or result of a country gradually reducing restrictions on the import of foreign goods and services, in an effort to promote free trade among different countries.

    Translation: 单边（贸易）自由化

3. multilateral trade

    Definition: Multilateral trade refers to trade under trade rules and regulatory mechanisms agreed between governments. These trade rules and regulation mechanisms are not applicable to trade between any one signatory country and other non-signatory countries. For example, the trade carried out by countries in the World Trade Organization belongs to multilateral trade.

    Translation: 多边贸易

4. quota

    Definition: A quota is the limited number or quantity of commodities which are officially allowed by trading parties.

    Translation: 定额，配额

5. public health

    Definition: Public health refers to preventing disease, prolonging life and promoting health through the organised efforts and informed choices of society, organisations, public and private, communities and individuals.

    Translation: 公共健康，公共卫生

Task 9

Suggested answer

When commodities reach maturity stage, the market gets saturated or the market growth tends to slow down. Although products have been accepted by most potential buyers, profit gradually declines after reaching its peak. At the same time, the market gets competitive, so the company needs to invest a lot in maintaining its product status, which will pose enormous challenges to its capital chain.